MONTU

Great Verses of the Bible

Photographers: The New Media Bible: cover, 14, 30, 39, 81, 90. Shostal Associates Inc.: 48 (M. Williams/Shostal), 64 (Kurt Scholz/Shostal), 72 (G. Nalbandian/Shostal). Stockphotos, Inc.: 23 (John R. Hamilton/Globe), 57 (H. Lentz/Globe).

Brownlow Publishing Company, Inc.
6309 Airport Freeway
Fort Worth, Texas 76117

A Special Gift

To

Ed and
Becky

From

The DeVargas
Family

Dec. 25th _____ 19 85

Great Verses of the Bible

F. B. MEYER

BROWNLOW PUBLISHING COMPANY, INC.

FORT WORTH, TEXAS

Brownlow Gift Books

Flowers That Never Fade
Flowers of Friendship
Flowers for You
Flowers for Mother
A Father's World
Better Than Medicine — A Merry Heart
Making the Most of Life — From A to Z
A Time to Laugh — or Grandpa Was a Preacher
Thoughts of Gold in Words of Silver
With the Good Shepherd
Living With the Psalms
The Story of Jesus
For Love's Sake
Today Is Mine
Leaves of Gold
Young in Heart
Rainbows
Windows
Daybreak
In His Steps
Some Quiet Place
Peace Be With You
The Fruit of the Spirit
Great Verses of the Bible
The Greatest Thing in the World
The More Years the More Sunshine
University of Hard Knocks

Contents

III. Great Verses of the New Testament

Introduction

"None of my books is dearer to me than this," said F. B. Meyer as he concluded the five volume series of devotional essays, *Our Daily Homily,* from which these messages have been selected and edited.

During the three years of writing, Meyer said he was consistently guided by "the reality of the unseen; the nearness of God; the duty and blessedness of doing all God commands, and bearing all He permits." It is no wonder that he ranks among the truly great Bible expositors of the nineteenth century — and the twentieth. For man's inner needs never cease or become outdated. Thus these devotionals addressed to humanity's well-being are as practical now as ever.

Meyer was a prolific writer, authoring more than seventy books. The depth and timelessness of his Biblical insight is evidenced by the fact that more than thirty of his works are still in print by numerous publishers.

As expected, some of the verses each person learned and recited in youth are not given in this edition. But all the ones included are truly *great verses,* especially when considered in the light of Meyer's scholarly and inspirational commentary. It is almost impossible to read these devotionals without being renewed by the majesty of God, by the strength of His love, by the power of His word.

It is understandable why that a hundred years ago a grateful public responded overwhelmingly to these essays. However, we believe these messages will do even more good in their second century of service and ministry than they did in their first.

And now — for the needs these messages may continue to fill, for the hurts they may heal, for the comfort they may bring, we send them with prayerful anticipation. As F. B. Meyer said, "To Him be the glory, who still multiples the five barley loaves and two small fish."

Paul C. Brownlow

Memories of Eden

The Lord God put him into the Garden. Genesis 2:15

THUS God started man in an ideal home. Memories of Eden, exquisite as dreams, weave the background of human life. Fellowship with the Creator, who walked its glades; its river, trees, and fruits; its blessed companionship; its light and noble toils — how fair the picture!

The Garden of Eden. That was God's ideal. When men point you to the scars on the world's face, left by the trail of the barbaric slaver, the march of the army, the decaying glory of human civilization, and ask how such things are consistent with God's love, you can point to that garden and say, "That is what the love of God meant for man; Satan and sin have wrought this."

The Garden of Gethsemane. Another garden was made necessary by the fall of man in the former garden. When man forfeited Eden, the Savior was revealed to regain it. He trod the winepress alone in the shadowed garden of the olive trees, that through its glades He might pass to His cross, and so make the wastes of sin bloom again as Eden. Is it wonderful that another Paradise is possible, when He sowed its seeds and watered the soil with His blood?

Turning Wastes into Gardens. In Eden man began as God's fellow-worker; and we now are called each day to do something towards reconstructing the Lost Paradise. Find your part in sowing, watering, or tending the tender shoots! Seek that your heart should be an Eden, kept sacred for the King, and endeavor your best to plant gardens where sandwastes and thorn-thickets have prevailed. Then, "instead of the thorn shall come up the fir tree, and instead of the briar shall come up the myrtle tree; and it shall be to the Lord for a name, for an everlasting sign" (Isaiah 55:11).

Promise in the Rainbow

*I set my bow in the cloud, and it shall be a token of a covenant
between me and the earth.* Genesis 9:13

A COVENANT is a promise or undertaking, resting on
certain conditions, with a sign or token attached to it. The
rainbow on the raincloud, the Lord's Supper, the wedding
ring, are signs and seals of the respective covenants to which
they belong. Whenever we see them we should think of the
covenant. Whenever you see a rainbow, remember the covenant God has made with us. For as He has sworn that the
water of Noah should no more cover the earth, so His kind-
ness shall not depart from us, nor the covenant of His peace
be removed. Three things are needed to make a rainbow.

A Cloud. Likewise, when man's sin overshadowed
Paradise, the bow of promise shone; and when the
thunderclouds gathered about the Savior's path, the Divine
Voice assured Him that as He had glorified the divine name
by His life, He should glorify it much more by His death.
When the black clouds of conviction, bereavement and
anguish beset us, look for the bow; it is always there,
though we do not always perceive it.

Rain. There are no rainbows unless there be falling drops
to catch and unravel the sunbeams. It may be that all suffering is worse in its anticipation than in its endurance; but
this is certain, that the big drops of sorrow have to patter
on our souls before we can realize all that God is prepared
to be to us.

Sunshine. It is only when God comes into our grief that
we can see the treasures of Love and Grace which are stored
for us in Him. We never know how great a blessing sorrow may be till we carry it into the light of the King's face.

Knowing the Almighty

I am God Almighty; walk before me and be thou perfect. Genesis 17:1

GOD precedes His commands with such revelations of Himself, that obedience is rendered easily possible. Before calling Abram to perfection, He described himself as *El Shaddai*, the Almighty. What may we accomplish if we learn to avail ourselves of the all-might of God? Oh to know the exceeding greatness of His power toward us who believe! Our lack is that we do not know our God, and therefore fail to perform exploits. "Thus saith the Lord, Let not the wise man glory in his wisdom, neither let the mighty man glory in his might, let not the rich man glory in his riches; but let him that glorieth glory in this, that he understandeth and knoweth Me." Let God talk with us and tell us the conditions on which He will make us exceedingly fruitful.

There must be wholeness in our surrender. No part of our nature can be barred or curtained off from God. Every chamber must be freely placed at His disposal; every relationship placed under His direction; every power devoted to His service. All we have and are must be entirely His.

There must be wholeness in our intention. The one aim of our Lord was to bring glory to His Father; and we should never be satisfied till we are so absolutely eager for the glory of Christ that we would seek it even at the cost of infamy to ourselves; and be as glad for another to bring it to Him, as we should be in bringing it ourselves.

There must be wholeness in our obedience. It was clearly so with Abram. As soon as God finished talking with His servant, he took Isaac and performed the rite which had just been enjoined.

Sunset over the Sea of Galilee

God Provides

And Abraham called the name of that place Jehovah-jireh;
in the mount of the Lord it shall be provided.   Genesis 22:14

ABRAHAM knew it would be. Probably he never told Sarah what God had asked of him till he and the lad were safely back in the tent. What need to trouble her? It was with an unfaltering tone that the patriarch told his young men that both of them would presently return. Even though he should actually take Isaac's life, he was sure that he would receive him again from the altar in health. It was only at the very last moment that God indicated the ram would be the sufficient substitute. So God's deliverances always come; they are provided in the mount of trial and sacrifice.

When the foe seemed secure of victory, God provided for the children of Israel. Pharaoh with his hosts counted on an easy victory, with the precipices around and the sea in front. To the eye of sense it seemed impossible to escape; all hope died. It was then that the Almighty parted the waters and made a path through the mighty deep.

In the fourth hour of the night, God provided for the disciples. Strength was well-nigh exhausted in the long battling with the waves. For hours the disciples with difficulty had kept themselves afloat. It seemed as if they must give in through physical collapse. It was then that Jesus drew nigh unto the ship as their rescuer.

So you may have come to the end of your own strength and wisdom and energy. The altar, wood, and fire are ready; the knife upraised; your Isaac set to die. But even now God will provide. Trust Him to provide the way of escape.

Victory in Defeat

He touched the hollow of his thigh.   Genesis 32:25

OUR greatest victories are wrought through pain, and purchased at the cost of the humbling of the flesh. Jacob learned that the secret of prevailing with God and man was not in strength, but in the weakness and suffering of the flesh. It must ever be so.

Had Laban met Jacob that morning, he would have pointed to that limp as an indication of God's wrath and displeasure. But if he had looked in Jacob's face, he would have seen all the hardness and cunning gone, and would have been amazed at the uncommon tenderness in his voice.

The shrunken sinew counteracts pride. Such a high spiritual achievement as wrestling with God might have tempted Jacob to arrogance and self-esteem. But God anticipated and prevented the possible temptation by this physical infirmity.

The shrunken sinew was the secret of victory. Had it not been shriveled by the angel's touch, Jacob would have continued to resist in the pride of his strength, and would never have clung convulsively to the angel, crying, "I will not let thee go." It was only in that act that Jacob became Israel, the Prince.

The shrunken sinew makes us think less of this world and more of the next. From this moment Jacob takes up more of the pilgrim attitude. He finds that for him, at least, the pace will have to be slower; but it is well, for he relaxes his hold on the seen to entwine more tenaciously about the unseen.

The Deeper Meanings of God

You meant it for evil, but God meant it for good. Genesis 50:20

GOD's deeper meanings! We are likely to see a malicious meaning; are we equally able to detect the divine and benevolent one? Our enemies are many, and they hate us with spiteful hatred; they are ever laying their plots, and working their unholy purposes. But there is a greater and wiser than they, who, through all these plottings, is prosecuting His divine purpose. There is another and deeper meaning than appears to the short sight of sense.

Let us believe that there is a divine and deeper meaning in adversities. Joseph might be forgiven for not doing so; but with his history and that of many others before us, we have no excuse for despair in the face of crushing sorrow. Whether it comes from man or devil, all creatures are under divine control holding to our lips the cup which the Father's hand has mixed. He has no complicity with their evil, but they unconsciously perform His will. Even if you cannot see the divine meaning, dare to believe that it is there.

Await the disclosures of time. Even in this life we sometimes reach a point from which we detect the meaning of the path by which we have been led. It may have been rough and difficult, but there was a reason in it all. Often God rewards our patient trust by allowing us in this life to see and know His purposes.

Await the full revelation of eternity. One day God will call us to His side in the clear light of eternity, and will explain His meanings in life's most sorrowful experiences. Then we shall learn that we suffered, not for ourselves only, but for others, and as part of His great remedial scheme, "to bring many unto salvation."

For the Praise of His Glory

The Egyptians shall know that I am the Lord. Exodus 7:5

IN God's dealings with His people, He purposed to reveal Himself to Egypt; so that when He led forth Israel's hosts, in redemption power from the brickfields of slavery on to freedom ground, there would be such a display of His love and pity and power, as the world had never before witnessed. Egypt and all surrounding nations would know the character of God in the Exodus, as the Lover and Redeemer of His own.

So with the Church. The Apostle tells us that redeemed men are the subjects of angelic contemplation and wonder. In the Church, principalities and powers shall discern the manifold wisdom and grace of God. When God has brought all the ransomed hosts up from the bondage of the world to stand in the radiance of the eternal morning, then the universe shall ring with the ascription, "Great and marvelous are thy works. Righteous and true are thy ways."

So with each individual believer. Each one of us has been formed for Jesus Himself, that we might show forth the praise of His glory (Ephesians 1:12). In growing purity and sweetness, in our deliverance from the clinging corruptions of the world and flesh, in our patience under tribulation, our submission and steadfast hope, in our willingness to sacrifice ourselves for others, let us be revelations of what Christ is, and of what He can make sinful men become.

Believers are the world's Bibles; by studying them, men may come to know the Lord Himself. Let us see to it that we are clear in type, unmistakable in our testimony, pleasant to behold, thoughtful and helpful towards all, commending the blessed Bridegroom whom the world sees not.

His Strong Hand

By strength of hand the Lord brought us out from Egypt, from the house of bondage. Exodus 13:14

FOUR times over in this chapter, Moses lays stress on the strong hand with which God redeemed His people from the bondage of Egypt; and we are reminded of "the exceeding greatness of His power, which is to us-ward who believe" (Ephesians 1:12-20).

God's strong hand reaches down to where we are. It would have been useless if Israel had been urged to help itself up to a certain point devoid of God's help. The people were so broken that they could only lie at the bottom of the pit, and moan. God's hand reached down to touch and grasp them at their lowest. When we are without strength, when we have expended our all in vain, when heart and flesh fail—then God comes where we are, and becomes the strength of our heart and our portion forever.

God's strong hand is mightier than our mightiest adversaries. Pharaoh was strong, and held the people as a child may hold a moth in its clenched fist. But a man's hand is stronger than a child's, and God's stronger than Pharaoh's. So Satan may have held you in bondage; but do not fear him any more, look away to the strength of God's hand. What can it not do for you?

We must appropriate and depend on God's strong hand. It is there next to us who believe, as a locomotive may be next to a line of railway cars; yet there must be a coupling-iron connecting them. So you must trust God's strength, and avail yourself of it, and yield to it. Remember that His arm is not shortened, nor His hand paralyzed, except as our unbelief and sin intercept and hinder the mighty working of His power.

Mine Own Possession

If ye will obey my voice and keep my covenant, then ye shall be mine own possession from among all peoples.   Exodus 19:5

OUR Savior told of a man who, in ploughing his field, heard his plough-share chink against buried treasure, and hastened to sell all that he had in order to buy it. In speaking thus, He pictured Himself as well as us. He found us before we found Him. The treasure is His people; to purchase them He gave up all that He had, even His throne (Matthew 13:44). "Ye are an elect race, a royal priesthood, a holy nation, a people for God's own possession, that ye may show forth the excellencies of Him who called you out of darkness into his marvelous light" (I Peter 2:9).

Where his treasure is, there is a man's heart. If it is in ships on the treacherous sea, he tosses restlessly on his bed, concerned for its safety. If it is in fabrics, he guards against moth; if in metal, against rust and thieves. And is Christ less careful for His own? Does He not guard with equal care against all that would deteriorate our value in His esteem? Need we fear the thief? Will not the Only-begotten keep us, so that the evil one shall not touch us (Matthew 6:19,20)?

God's treasure is His. "They shall be mine, saith the Lord of Hosts, in the day that I do make, even a peculiar treasure." He will hold his own, as men cling to their treasure, binding it about their loins, in a storm at sea.

Let us remember the conditions: to obey His voice, and keep His covenant; then on eagles' wings He will bring us to Himself. Compliance with these is blessed in its results. God regards us with the ecstasy of a love that rejoices over us with singing; and looks on us as a mother on her child, a miser on his gold.

The Scapegoat

*And the goat shall bear upon him all their iniquities unto a
solitary land.* Leviticus 16:22

THIS chapter is full of Christ in His most precious death
for men. Its various aspects are set forth under these diverse
sacrifices, as light reflected from the many facets of a dia-
mond. As we consider the goat which was led away into
the wilderness, we see in it the following:

Christ made sin for us. With both hands Aaron, in sym-
bol, transferred all the iniquities, sins, and transgressions of
the people to the head of the goat, which became so iden-
tified with sin that it was accounted an unclean thing. Even
he who led it away must wash his clothes and bathe. This
is what the Apostle Paul means when he says that Jesus was
made sin for us. Our sins met in Him; were assumed by
Him; He stood before God as though, in some mysterious
sense, they were His own.

Christ bearing sin away. As the goat went away, the eyes
of the people followed it, and they were taught to believe
that sin was no longer reckoned to them. Aaron put off his
linen garments and arrayed himself in festival robes, and
came forth to bless the congregation. What rejoicing must
have broken from the crowds! So Jesus, in his matchless
grace, has borne away the sin of the world into a land of
forgetfulness. "Their sins and iniquities will I remember no
more."

Christ's loneliness. He was alone in His mediatorial work.
None could bear Him company. Loved ones might stand
beside His cross, or in later ages suffer, as He did, deaths
of martyrdom. But none could do what He did as the
sacrifice for sin. How lonely He was! Even the Father
seemed to have forsaken Him!

He Dwelt Among Them

Without the camp . . . in the midst whereof I dwell.
Numbers 5:3

WHAT a sublime conception! God dwelt with His people. The Tabernacle was His tent among theirs; the cloudy pillar was His emblem. To attack the Israelites was to come into collision with Him. All the expense and anxiety of the march rested on His shoulders, as the care of a family of young children on a father. How important it was for nothing to grieve or offend Him!

What the camp of Israel was in those long-ago days, the Church is now. It is the host of the redeemed, the representative of God, the pilgrimage of the saints. Among His people God still walks, and dwells, and tabernacles (John 1:14). Their griefs, conflicts, and experiences are shared by their ever present Almighty Friend.

The presence of God in the Church is by the Holy Spirit. "Know ye not that ye are the temple of God, and that the Spirit of God dwelleth in you?" (I Corinthians 3:16; 6:19). He is with her and in her as the Body of which the risen Lord is Head.

How careful we must be in the conduct of our church-life, as well as our individual lives, so that there may be nothing to offend Him! "What will our God think of this?" should be always our first inquiry. We must walk "in the fear of the Lord and in the comfort of the Holy Spirit," if we would be edified and multiplied, as were the churches throughout Judaea and Galilee, and Samaria (Acts 9:31).

The city of Jerusalem

Heirs of God

Thou shalt have no inheritance in their land. I am thy portion and thine inheritance among the children of Israel.
Numbers 18:20.

WE are God's portion, and He is ours. The Lord's portion is His people; Israel is the lot of His inheritance. We, with all we have, for God; and God, with all He has, for us. "Heirs of God."

We are like settlers on the fringe of their estate. The emigrant to the far west had a plot of land allotted to him, but how little did he know of its contents! There might have been coal, or iron ore, or rivers full of fish, or rich soil. He settled on the outskirts, but every year he pushed his fences farther back to take in more of the land, which was all his, but it was not yet brought into use or under cultivation. So each year we should increase in the knowledge of who God is, and of what He is willing to be to us. Not as though we were already perfect; but we follow on to apprehend that for which we were apprehended, and to be filled full with His grace and heavenly benediction.

Our possession of God will largely depend on his possession of us. There are some who wonder that God is so much more to others than to them. Is not the answer to be found in their withholding so much of what they might yield up to His occupation and use? If you would have all from God, you must give all to God. Your enjoyment of God will be in precise proportion to the deepening and widening consecration of your life.

Why should any of us be poor, or strengthless, or fearful, when all the Godhead is stored in Jesus, and awaits our appropriation? Go up and possess His infinite continent that flows with milk and honey, watered by the rain of heaven and rich in treasure.

The Harvest of Sin

Ye have sinned against the Lord and be sure your sin will find you out. Numbers 32:23.

SIN is like the boomerang of the savage; it comes back on the hand that launched it forth. Joseph's brothers were envious of him and cast him into a pit; later they were cast into prison by Joseph. King David committed adultery and murder; so Absalom requited him. The Jews crucified the blessed Lord; and they were later impaled around Jerusalem by the Romans till room and wood for their crosses failed.

There is a divine order in society. God has so constituted the world, that as man deals with his neighbor, so he is dealt with. The consequence does not always follow immediately. There is often a long interval between the lightning flash and the thunderpeal. The sentence against an evil work is not executed suddenly. But though God's mills grind slowly, they do grind, and to powder. It is impossible to deceive God; for His immutable law says, "whatsoever a man soweth, that shall he also reap. For he that soweth to his flesh shall of the flesh reap corruption; but he that soweth to the Spirit shall of the Spirit reap life everlasting" (Galatians 6:7,8).

When sin comes to find you out, like a bloodhound on the track of the criminal, be sure that it finds you in Jesus. "That I may be found in Him." Nothing will avail to intercept the awful execution of sin's vengeance, except the blood and righteousness of Jesus. Put Him between you and your sins, between you and your past, between you and the penalty of a broken law.

On Eagles' Wings

*As an eagle stirreth up her nest, fluttereth over her young
. . . and beareth them on her wing.* Deuteronomy 32:11

THREE references are made to the eagle in this passage.

She stirs up her nest. When her fledglings are old enough
to fly, but linger around the few bits of stick, dignified as
a nest, the mother bird breaks it up, and scatters them. How
much better this, than that they should miss the luxury of
flight on outspread wings in the blue vault, and of basking
in the eye of the sun. So when the Father sees His children
clinging to earth's bare rocks, captured and held by the poor
sticks they have gathered, and missing the glory of living,
He breaks up the nest. The fortune is dispersed, the home
broken up, the aspect of life changed. We are then able to
enjoy the bliss of life in the heavenlies with Christ Jesus.

She flutters over her young. They stand scared and
wretched on the edge of the rock, but she glides gently
above them, now edging around, now mounting, then drop-
ping far below to rise again. She allures them to follow her
example. Here again we have an emblem of God's efforts
to make us imitators of Himself, to teach us the possibilities
that await us in Jesus.

She spreads forth her wings and takes them. Incited by
the mother's endeavors, the eaglet may venture on the un-
tried air, and lo! the unaccustomed wings fail beneath its
weight. It falls, but not far, for the mother swoops beneath,
and bears it up and away. Trembling soul, God is beneath
you. If your faith fails, and you are falling, like another
Peter, into a bottomless abyss, He will catch you and bear
you up, and teach you the mystery of the more abundant
life.

Unfailing Promises

There failed not aught of any good thing which the Lord had
spoken. Joshua 21:45

SUCH will be the summary of our lives, as we review
them from the land of the sunset. We shall see plenty of our
own failures, shortcomings, and sins, and sadly acknowledge
them. We shall see that our unbelief and disobedience
deprived us of enjoying much that God intended for us. We
shall see that whatever was lacking was in no wise due to
Him, but to ourselves. The land of our inheritance was
given to us in Jesus; but we suffered the lack of much,
because of our failure to enter in.

There may be long delays in the fulfillment of promise.
But delays are not denials; and it is better to let the fruit
ripen before you pluck it. Wait till God drops it into your
hand; it will be ever so much sweeter.

There may be enemies and obstacles. But they will fall
back, before the will of God, as the gates of night roll back
before the touch of dawn. Do not scheme or fret or be im-
patient. God is doing all to make our life full of favor and
blessing. Wait on Him and keep His way. He will exalt us
to inherit the earth. Obedient to Him, we are as safe as if
the gate of pearl was behind us; our joy cannot rust or be
stolen; every wind is a south wind; every shore our native
land; every circumstance a rough packing-crate containing
the gifts of our Father's love.

There may be ignorance and weakness. But God can
deal with this also. Take Him your imperfect apprehension,
your faltering faith, He can make right what is wrong, and
help you to receive all He waits to give. Heaven will be full
of wonder at the way in which God has kept His word, and
done all that He promised — and more.

Our Need for a Priest

Dwell with me, and be unto me a father and a priest.
Judges 17:10

MEN crave for a priest. In every age of the world's history there has been an altar indicating man's consciousness of God, and a priest suggesting man's consciousness of unworthiness to enter into the Divine presence. Man has perpetually taken one of his fellows whose character seemed less blemished than that of others, and after setting him apart with special rites from the ordinary engagements of life, has promised him maintenance and honor, if only he will act as priest. Be my priest; say for me to God what I cannot say. The sacrifices offered by your hands are more likely to reach Him than those rendered by mine.

Let us beware of the religion which ignores man's craving for a priest. The world abounds with attempts at religious systems, from which the conception of the priest is eliminated. These reduce the worship of God to a system of noble thinking, but fail to deal with man's consciousness of sin and his yearning for a settled basis of peace.

Let us remember that all human priests must ultimately fail. God has put them all aside, setting up the priesthood of the blessed Lord. "We have such a High Priest, who is set on the right hand of the throne of the Majesty in the heavens; a minister of the sanctuary, and of the true tabernacle which the Lord pitched, and not a man." Stars are needless when the sun has arisen. The human priesthood is rendered unnecessary since the Son of God has passed into the heavens to be a priest after the order of Melchizedek. Now no one has a right to pose as priest to others, except in the sense that all Christians are priests to each other.

God Is Here

Who is this Philistine, that he should defy the armies of the living God? I Samuel 17:26

THIS made all the difference between David and the rest of the camp. To Saul and his soldiers, God was an absentee — a name, but little else. They believed that He had done great things for His people in the past, and that at some future time, in the days of the Messiah, He might be expected to do great things again. But no one thought of Him as present. Keenly sensitive to the defiance of the Philistine, and grieved by the apathy of God's people, David on the other hand, felt that God was alive. He had lived alone with Him in the solitude of the hills, until God had become one of the greatest and most real facts of his young existence; and as the lad went to and fro among the armed warriors, he was sublimely conscious of the presence of the living God amid the clamor of the camp.

This is what we need: to live so much with God, that when we are among men, whether in the bazaars of India or the marketplace of our own town, we may be more aware of His overshadowing presence than of the presence or absence of any one. Lo, God is here! This place is hallowed ground! But none can realize this by the act of the will. We can only find God everywhere when we carry Him everywhere. The coal miner sees by the candle he carries on his forehead.

Each of us is opposed by difficulties, privations, and trials of different sorts. But the one answer to them all is faith's vision of the Living God. We can face the mightiest foe in His name. If our faith can but make Him a passage, along which He shall come, there is no Goliath He will not quell; no question He will not answer; no need He will not meet.

Ancient road in Israel

Made Great by Gentleness

Thy gentleness hath made me great. II Samuel 22:36

THE triumph of God's gentle goodness will be our song forever. In those far distant ages, when we look back on our earthly course, as a grown man on his boyhood, we shall recognize that the Hand which brought us thither was as gentle as our mother's; and that the things we craved, but failed to receive, were withheld by His gentle goodness. Our history tells what gentleness will do.

The Apostle besought the Corinthian converts by the gentleness of Christ (II Corinthians 10:1). Though there were abuses among them that seemed to call for stringent dealing, Paul felt they could be best removed by the gentle love which he had learned from the heart of Christ. The wisdom which is from above is gentle as well as pure; and in dealing with the sin that chokes our growth, it is probable that gentleness will do more than severity. The gentleness of the nurse that cherishes her children; of the lover to her whom he cherishes above himself; of the infinite love which bears and endures to the uttermost — this gentleness is the furnace before which the foul ingredients of our hearts are driven never to return. We might brave the lion; we are vanquished by the Lamb. We could withstand the scathing look of scorn; but when the gentle Lord casts on us the look of tenderness, we go out to weep bitterly.

That He has borne with us so lovingly; that He has filled our lives with mercy even when compelled to correct; that He has never altered in His tender behavior towards us; that He has returned our rebuffs and slights with meekness and forbearance; that He has never wearied of us — this is an everlasing tribute to the gentleness that makes great.

The Cost of Love

*Neither will I offer burnt offerings unto the Lord my God of
that which doth cost me nothing. II Samuel 24:24*

GOD'S love for us cost Him something. He spared not
His own Son, and that Son spared not His blood. But how
little our love to Him costs us! Let us understand that where
there is true, strong love to Jesus, it will cost us something.
Love is the costliest of all undertakings.

Love will cost us Self-denial. Christ and self are perfect-
ly incompatible; to have the one we must be prepared to
surrender the other. The heart subtly schemes to hold both;
but it does not deceive Christ. He knows in a moment when
we have preferred to spare ourselves and to sacrifice Him,
or to obey Him and sacrifice ourselves. We know it also.
At first we may find it difficult to count all things but loss
for Him; but as we go on doing it, as we see the smile of
pleasure on His face, our hearts leap with joy, and we love
to give Him everything. We give everything not thinking of
the cóst, any more than Mary did when she broke the
alabaster box of very precious ointment. After all, it is but
fitting that we offer our bodies "a living sacrifice, holy, ac-
ceptable unto God."

Love will cost us Companionships. Those who knew us
will pass us and look the other way. It will cost us hard-
earned money; for we shall realize that we have no property
in anything that we possess. It will cost us respect and
repute among our fellows. But what shall we mind if we
gain Christ? We cannot give up for Him without regaining
everything we have renounced, but now it is purified and
transfigured. Did not the Lord say so? And did He not add
a hundredfold, with persecution. Let us heartily respond.
"Lord, Thou knowest all things: Thou knowest that I love
Thee!"

Hallowed Temples

*I have heard thy prayer and thy supplication . . . I have
hallowed this house which thou hast built. I Kings 9:3*

MAN builds; God hallows. This cooperation between man
and God pervades all life. Man performs the outward and
mechanical; God the inward and spiritual. Paul plants,
Apollos waters; but God gives the increase. We elaborate
our sermons and addresses, building them up with careful,
eager thought; but God must work in and through them for
His own glory in the salvation and upbuilding of souls. We
must be careful to do our part with reverence and godly
fear, remembering that God must work in realms we cannot touch, and to issues we cannot reach, before our poor
exertions can avail.

*May we not apply this especially to the education of a
child's life?* Many who read these lines are engaged in
building structures that will outlive the pyramids. The body
is only the scaffolding, behind and through which the
building of the soul is taking place. The materials with
which we build may be the gold, silver, and precious stones,
of our example, precept, careful watching, and discipline;
but God must come in to hallow. Our strenuous endeavor
must be supplemented by the presence of the Heavenly
Father.

God hallows by His indwelling. Holiness is the result of
His putting His Name into a place, a day, a human soul;
for His Name is His nature, Himself. Each day may be a
building, reared between sunrise and sunset, with our activities; but we cannot hope to realize our ideal unless the
structure becomes a temple filled with God. Build what you
will; but never be satisfied unless God sets His eyes and
heart upon your life, hallowing and sanctifying each day
and act to Himself.

Where God Wants Us

I have commanded the ravens to feed thee . . . behold, I have commanded a widow to sustain thee. I Kings 17:4,9

WE must be where God desires. Elijah spoke of himself as always standing before the Lord God of Israel. He deemed himself as much a prince in the royal palace as Gabriel (Luke 1:19). And he could as distinctly stand before God when hiding beside Cherith, or living in the widow's house at Zarephath, as when he stood erect on Carmel, or listened to the voice of God at Horeb. Wherever you go, and whatever ministry you are called to undertake, glory in this — that you never go to any greater distance from God.

If we are where God wants us to be, He will see to the supply of our need. It is as easy for Him to feed us by the ravens as by the widow. As long as God says, stay here, or there, be sure that He is pledged to provide for you. Though you resemble a lonely sentinel in some distant post of missionary service, God will see to you. The ravens are no less guided by His command than of old; and out of the stores of widows He is able to supply your need as He did Elijah's, at Zarephath.

How often God teaches best in seclusion and solitude. It is beside the murmuring brooks of nature that we have our deepest lessons. It is in the homes of the poor that we are fitted for our greatest tasks. It is beside couches where children suffer and die, that we receive those preparations of the heart which avail us when the bugle note summons us to some difficult post.

All His Wondrous Works

Sing psalms unto him, talk ye of all his wondrous works.
I Chronicles 16:9

WE do not talk sufficiently about God. Why it is so may not be easy to explain; but there seems too much silence among Christian people about the best things. In the days of Malachi, "they that feared the Lord spake often one to another, and the Lord hearkened and heard." We talk about sermons, details of worship and church organization, or the latest phase of Scripture interpretation. We discuss men, methods, and churches; but our talk in the home and in Christian gatherings is too seldom about the wonderful works of God. Better to speak less, and to talk more of Him.

Probably the real cause of our avoidance of this best of topics is that our hearts are filled with so much which is not of God, and they speak out of their abundance. You may judge the contents of a shop by what is in the windows; and you may judge the inner life of Christians by the subjects which are most familiar to their lips. Our hearts do not seek for God and His strength, nor His face continually; and therefore we find it hard to talk of all His wondrous works.

What God has done in the past, as recorded on the page of Scripture; what He is doing day by day in the world around, and in our hearts; what He has promised to do when He comes again — these are the themes His children need to discuss.

The Sufficient One

Be strong and of good courage, for the Lord God will be with thee; he will not fail thee, nor forsake thee. I Chronicles 28:20

IT is very comforting to take these words to our hearts; especially when we connect them with the foregoing ones about the pattern, and apply the whole passage to the temple-building of our own lives. For each of us there is a pattern, an ideal, a design, based on the possibilities which God sees to be within our reach. For each of us there is an abundance of stored provision; but we are not always strong to do. In Jesus there is the complete ideal of human life; of the Child at Nazareth; of the Servant in the workshop; of the Lover in His affection for His church; of the Friend, the Sufferer, the Patriot, the Savior. Go forth and imitate Him!

Sometimes our heart and flesh fail us in the mid-passage of life. Once the energy and vigor of youth promised to sustain and carry us to the end of life, without fear or failure. But these die down, and we wonder how the remainder of our life plan can be fulfilled. And the one sufficient answer is — God. He who helped our fathers to the very end will help us. He who did not fail or forsake them, will never leave nor forsake us, until all the work of life which He has planned is finished.

You will do better and more enduring work henceforth than you have ever done in the heyday and abundance of youthful power, if you let God work all through you to His own glory. You have no need for despondency, God is sufficient. Oh to write this down on the tablets of our heart — God is; God is here; God is all-sufficient; God has begun and will finish! God has promised that He will never leave nor forsake us. Therefore we may boldly say, "God is my helper, I will not fear what man shall do unto me."

Wisdom and Riches

*Because thou hast not asked riches, wealth, or honor, but hast
asked for wisdom and knowledge, wisdom and knowledge is
granted unto thee; and I will give thee riches.*

II Chronicles 1:11,12

SOLOMON had chosen wisdom and knowledge that he
might honor God in the sight of His people. And in return
God honored him, and supplemented his choice with abundant wealth.

This reminds us of the constant teaching of Jesus. He who
seeks his life loses it; but to lose it is to save it in the best
and deepest sense. Seek first the kingdom of God and His
righteousness, and all these things shall be added (Matthew
6:33).

*The conception of life given in the Bible differs marked-
ly from the maxims and practices of some good and earnest
people.* Their notion is that materials come first, that they
must work for their living, "keep the wolf from the door,"
and educate their children. These objects are legitimate; but
they were never meant by God to be the supreme aim of
His servants.

His object in our creation, redemption, and regeneration,
was that we might serve His redemptive purposes in the
world, manifest His character, do His will, win souls for His
kingdom, administer the gifts with which He had entrusted
us. He asks us to rise to this high calling, and give our
whole life to its realization. He will be responsible for all
else. It is surely His will that we should give ourselves to
useful trades, and fill our days with honest toil; but the
main purpose should ever be His glory, and the exemplifica-
tion in word and act of His holy character. If we ask for
wisdom to do this well, we shall get all else in the bargain.

The Strength of Joy

The joy of the Lord is your strength.   Nehemiah 8:10

"THE sad heart tires in a mile," is a frequent proverb. What a difference between the energy of the healthy, joyous heart and the forced activity of the morbid and depressed one! The one leaps to its task, the other creeps to it. The one discovers its meat and drink in self-sacrifice, the other limps, and stoops, and crawls.

If you want to be strong for life's work, keep a glad heart. But, be equally sure you are glad with the joy of the Lord. There is a counterfeit of it in the world, of which we must beware — an outward merry-making, jesting, and excited laughter, which hides an aching and miserable heart. Solomon compared the joy of the world to the crackling of thorns under a pot, which flare up with great speed, but burn out before the water in the pot is warm.

Ours must be the joy of the Lord. It begins with the assurance of forgiveness and acceptance in the Beloved. It is nourished in trial and tribulation, which veil outward sources of consolation, and lead us to rejoice in God through our Lord Jesus. It is independent of circumstances, so that its possessors can sing in the stocks. It lives not in the gifts of God, but in God Himself. It is the fruit of the Spirit who begets in us love, joy, peace, long-suffering. Let the Lord Himself fill your soul, and joy will be as natural as the murmur of a brook to its flow.

And such joy will always reveal itself to others. You will desire to send portions to those for whom nothing is prepared. Your joy will be contagious; it will shed its kindly light on sad and weary hearts.

Sea of Galilee near Magdala

For Such a Time as This

WHAT grand faith was here! Mordecai was in God's
secrets, and was assured that deliverance and salvation
would come to his people from some quarter — if not from
Esther, then from some other. But he was extremely anxious that she should not miss the honor of being her people's savior. Therefore he suggested that she had come to
her high position for this very purpose.

*None of us know, at first, God's reasons for bringing us
into positions of honor and trust.* Why is that young girl
suddenly made head over that household? Why is that
youth taken from the ranks of working people, and placed
in the pulpit of that great church? Why is that man pro-
moted in his business, so that he is the head of the firm in
which he served as an office boy? All these are parts of the
divine plan. God has brought them to the Kingdom that He
may work out through them some great purpose of
salvation.

They have the option, however, to serve or not. They
may use their position for themselves, for their own
enhancement and enjoyment, that they may surround
themselves with strong fortifications against misfortune; but
in that case they court destruction. Their position and
wealth may vanish as suddenly as it came. Ill health and
disaster may overtake them.

If, on the other hand, all is used for God, even at the risk
of perishing — the issue is blessed. Those that love their
lives lose them; those that are prepared to forfeit them keep
them. Only the grain of wheat which is buried in the soil
bears much fruit.

My Servant Job

*Hast thou considered my servant Job, that there is none like him
in the earth, a perfect and an upright man.* Job 2:3

EVEN God spoke of Job as perfect. Not that he was absolutely so, as judged by the perfect standard of eternity,
but as judged by the standard of his own light and
knowledge. Job was living up to all the requirements of God
and man, so far as he understood them. His whole being
was open and obedient to the divine impulses. So far as he
knew there was no cause of controversy in heart or life.
Probably he could have adopted the words of the Apostle,
"I know nothing against myself."

Satan suggested that Job's goodness was pure selfishness;
that it paid him well to be as he was, because God had
hedged him around and blessed his substance. This malig-
nant suggestion was at once dealt with by the Almighty Vin-
dicator of the saints. It was as if God said, "I give thee permission to deprive him of all those favoring conditions, for
the sake of which thou sayest he is bribed to goodness; and
it shall be seen that his integrity is rooted deep down in the
work of my grace upon his heart."

In all this God desired to teach Job that there were flaws
and blemishes in his character which could only be seen by
comparing it with the more perfect glory of His own divine
nature. Job's friends sought to prove him faulty, and
failed; God revealed Himself, and he cried, "Behold, I am
vile, and abhor myself, and repent in dust and ashes."

How often God takes away our consolations, that we
may only love Him for Himself; and reveals our sinfulness,
that we may better appreciate the completeness of His
salvation!

Knowledge Builds Trust

They that know thy name will put their trust in Thee.
Psalm 9:10

WE do not trust, because we do not know. If we were once to know God, it would seem as absurd to doubt Him as to fear that we should fly off at a tangent from the surface of the earth. Men complain of their little faith. The remedy is in their own hands; let them set themselves to know God. We may know about God, and yet not know Him. We may hear what others say about Him, but have no direct and personal acquaintance.

The materials for the knowledge of God are all around us — make use of them. Think of the promises by which God has bound Himself to nurture those who come to Him; of the record of His gracious intercessions for His saints; of the necessity that He should maintain His character and reputation in the face of the universe.

Above all, believe as Jesus bade, from your own heart. Would you give stones to hungry babes, and scorpions into childish hands? Would you desert a forlorn and hunted soul that trusted? Would you insist on a certain measure of agony before stepping in to deliver? Would you take delight in inflicting needless anguish? And will God? Trust may be read as the superlative of true. To trust is to count God true, though circumstances belie; to count Him truer than the sentimental forebodings of our hearts; to count Him our truest and tenderest Friend. "Yet let God be true, though every man is proved to be a liar" (Romans 3:4).

But for all this, we must make time. We cannot know a friend in hurried interviews, much less God. So we must steep ourselves in deep, long thoughts of His nearness and His love.

Goodness and Mercy

Surely goodness and mercy shall follow me all the days of my life. Psalm 23:6

WE are well escorted, with a Shepherd in front and these twin angelic benefactors behind! We make such mistakes, give unnecessary pain, leave work ill-done and half-done, often succeed rather in raising dust than cleaning the rooms which we would sweep! It is good to remember that Goodness and Mercy follow close upon our track as we go through life, putting kind constructions on our actions, disentangling knots, making good deficiencies, and preventing the consequences of ill-advised and inconsiderate action from pursuing us to the bitter end.

There are mothers who are always tidying up after their children. The little ones have had a rare time, have left confusion and disorder; but the mother comes, mending the broken toys, stitching the torn garments, making everything neat and tidy. As the medical corps goes over the battlefield — as love puts the most tender construction on word and act — so the love of God follows us.

His goodness imputes to us the noble motive, though the act itself has been a failure; credits us with what was in our heart; gives us the full wage, though we have only toiled one hour. His mercy forgives, obliterates the traces of our sins from His heart, undoes their ill-effects so far as possible towards others, and treats us as if we had never transgressed. Do not fear the future. God's Goodness and Mercy do not tire. What has been will be, in all worlds, and to all eternity.

44

Who Bears Our Burdens

Blessed be the Lord, who daily beareth our burden. Psalm 68:19

NEVER tired or out of patience, our mighty God daily carries our burdens, and sets Himself to help us through the crushing difficulties. They are unbearable to us, but not to Him. If He takes up the worlds as a very little thing, surely our heaviest burden must be less.

But our mistake is we do not realize God is bearing our burdens. We think that we must cope with them. We let ourselves worry, as though we were the loneliest, most deserted, most pitiable beings in existence, when all the while God is going along beside, ready to bear our burdens. The burden of our sins; of our anxieties about ourselves, and about others; of our frailties and infirmities; the responsibility of keeping us; the pressure of our daily need — all these rest daily on our God.

Tis enough that He should care;
Why should we the burden bear!

Let us not carry our burdens for a single moment longer; pass them over to Him who has already taken our eternal interests to His heart. Only be patient, and wait on Him. Do not run to and fro seeking for help from man, or making men your consolers and confidants. Those who do have their reward. But as for you, anoint your head and wash your face, so as not to excite the pity of others. "Cast thy burden on the Lord, and He will sustain thee." But, when it has been cast, leave it with Him. Refuse to yield to anxious suggestions; burst out into a song of thankful confidence. Bless Him! Praise Him! Be glad, and rejoice! The heart lightened of its load will soar.

The Becoming One

*The Lord God is a sun and shield: the Lord will give grace and
glory.* Psalm 84:11

HOW God suits Himself to our need! In darkness, He is
a Sun; in the sultry noon, a Shield; in our earthly
pilgrimage He gives grace; when the morning of heaven
breaks, He will give glory. He suits Himself to every vary-
ing circumstance in life. He becomes what the demand of
the moment requires. And as the Psalmist well says, He
withholds no good thing from them that walk uprightly. Let
us learn the art of receiving from God.

The sun is the source of light and life. With impartial
goodness He scatters His beams on palace and cottage,
mountain summit and lowland vale. He is ever pouring out
His beams. It is our part only to stand in them, to open
a window or door. God is shining, dear heart. Get out of
thyself, and sun thy shivering frame in His untiring love.

*A shield may be the shadow of a great rock in the
scorching desert,* or the canopy of a gourd's growth. Put
God between yourself and the oppressive, hot winds of
temptation. Is the noon with its burning heat too much for
you? Hide in the Lord God. The heat shall not smite you
by day nor the frost by night.

Dost thou need Grace? He is full of it. His grace is sufficient. With both hands He will give and give again; only
practice the habit of taking. Grace is the bud of which
Glory is the flower. If He has given this, He will not
withhold that. If we knew the gift of God, we would be
sure that Glory in germ is within us, waiting only for the
summer of Eternity to develop in perfect beauty. "We have
had our access by faith into this grace wherein we stand,
and we rejoice in hope of the glory of God."

Ready to Forgive

Thou, Lord, art good, and ready to forgive. Psalm 86:5

WE are blinded by sin, and cannot believe that God is ready to forgive. We think we must induce Him to forgive us, by pleading and pleading and self-abasement, not knowing that He is ready to forgive. There is in every heart such difficulty in understanding the unwearying patience and ever-yearning love of our Heavenly Father. Clasp these words to your heart! Say them over and over again — "Ready to forgive, ready to forgive!"

At any moment of the sad history of the Prodigal, had he returned, he would have found his old father as ready to forgive as on the day, too long delayed, when he did return. The only pity was that he had not come long before.

We have fallen a hundred times, and are ashamed to come to God again; it seems too much to expect that He will receive us again. But He will, for He is ready to forgive. We feel that our sin is aggravated, because we knew so much better; but He is as ready to forgive us now as when first we came. We are disposed to wait a little, till our sin has become more remote, till passion has subsided, till the inscription has faded from the wall; but we might as well go at once, God is as ready to forgive at this moment as at any future time. We are wounding Him greatly by doubting Him. He is ready, waiting, eager to forgive. We have only to call upon Him and we will discover the plenteousness of His mercy. How ready Jesus ever was to forgive sinners, herein revealing God's heart!

> O Love, Thou deep eternal tide,
>   How dear are men to Thee!
> The Father's heart is opened wide
>   By Jesus' blood to me.

The Sheep of His Pasture

We are his; we are his people, and the sheep of his pasture.
Psalm 100:3

THE sense of God's proprietorship is the true basis of our consecration. We must realize His rights over us before we can freely give Him His due. Those rights are manifold in their sweet reasonableness; but among them all, this of creation is one of the chief. God has a right to us because He made us.

He made us, as the potter fashions the clay, for a distinct purpose; and surely He has a right to use the vessels of His workmanship for the purpose which He has designed them.

He made us, as the builder erects a house for the purpose of inhabiting it; and surely He has a right to occupy every distinct room, and go throughout it as He may please.

He made us, as the hand of the weaver makes some textile fabric for wearing; and surely He must not be debarred from the free and unquestioned disposal of that on which He has expended work and time.

We are Christ's by creation, by purchase, by the gift of the Father. The Good Shepherd owns us, though we do not always acknowledge His ownership, or repay His pains and wounds on our behalf. Look up into His face and say, "I am thine by a myriad ties, and am bound to Thee for evermore. Lead me where Thou wilt; guide me whither Thou choosest; count me as one of thy people; feed me on thy pasture lands; make as much of me as Thou canst, this side of heaven; number me with thy saints in glory everlasting." With bowed heads and open hearts, may we offer ourselves. We can do no more, and we dare do no less.

"Good Shepherd Hills" in Galilee

49

If the World My Savior Knew

Oh, praise the Lord, all ye nations!   Psalm 117:1

THIS is an unusual summons from Jewish lips. For the
most part the Jews looked with little sympathy on their
Gentile neighbors, and had no desire that they should laud
Jehovah, unless they became proselytes of Judaism. But
where the love of God is strong in the heart, it overleaps
the bounds of custom and racial prejudice, and yearns that
all the world should know and love the Savior.

> If all the world my Savior knew,
> Sure all the world would love Him too.

*We all need more of the emancipating power of the love
of Christ,* to thaw the icy chains that hang around us and
bid words flow freely from our lips to those we have
thought were outside the range of our influence. Oh, for the
passionate desire that God should be universally praised and
loved! Oh, if only we might inspire lips to praise Him that
otherwise had remained sealed!

Are we doing all we can to kindle the nations to praise?
They cannot praise Him whom they do not know. It is mere
hypocrisy to bid them praise Him, if we have never sought
to spread, by lip or gift, the mercy and truth revealed in
Jesus our Lord. Oh that we might ponder the paradox —

> Christ, alone, can save this world;
> But Christ cannot save this world, alone.

Divinely Directed

*Trust in the Lord with all thine heart; and lean not unto thine
own understanding. In all thy ways acknowledge him, and he
shall direct thy paths.* Proverbs 3:5,6

THY paths! Then, every man's path is distinct for him,
and for no other. The paths may lie side by side, but they
are different. They have converged; they may diverge. When
Peter had been told of the rugged nature of the path
marked out for him in the Providence of God, he turned
toward John, his companion and friend, and said to Jesus,
"What shall this man do?" The Lord instantly replied, in effect: "That is entirely a matter for my choice and will; if
I will, it may be that he shall tarry till I come."

We need to be divinely directed. The man who stands
above the maze can direct you through all its turns by the
readiest path. God who made thee for thy life, and thy life
for thee, can direct thee, and He only.

First: "Lean not to thine own understanding." We are apt
to pride ourselves on our far-sighted judgment. But we have
to learn that our own understanding is not keen enough or
wise enough to direct; we must renounce all dependence on
it.

Second: "In all thy ways acknowledge Him." Let our eye
be single; our one aim to please Him; our sole motive, His
glory. It is marvelous how certainly and delightfully our
way opens before us when we no longer look down on it,
or around at others, but simply upwards into the face of
Christ. It is a universal law, unalterable as the nature of
God, that no created being can be truly holy, useful, or
happy, who is knowingly and deliberately out of the divine
fellowship, for a single moment.

The Trustworthy Wife

The heart of her husband doth safely trust in her.
Proverbs 31:11

THIS alphabetical poem to godly womanhood is one of the gems of Old Testament Scriptures. Clearly the Hebrew woman was held in high honor, and had as much freedom of action as she enjoys in Christian countries. The contrast was very marked, compared to the women of other nations. But in the whole description there is hardly any trait more beautiful than this — absolute trustworthiness. We can see the pair together: the husband comes in from sitting among the elders, his heart weighted with affairs of state, and he seeks her confidence and advice. He has no fear of her betraying his secrets. He can safely trust her.

This surely is the most sacred joy a woman can have. To be consulted, to be trusted, to share the common toils and responsibilities. Who would not work willingly with her hands, and rise while yet night and engage in ceaseless toils, if only she had the inspiration that trust brings!

> If then your future life should need
>   A strength my love can only gain
> Through suffering — or my heart be freed
>   Only by sorrow from some stain,
> Then you shall give, and I will take
> This Crown of fire for Love's dear sake.

Can Christ, in like manner, safely trust us? Can He trust us with His secrets, His interests, His money? Abraham was one whom God could safely trust, and He did trust him as His friend: "Shall I hide from Abraham, . . . for I have known him?" Therefore, to be God's friend, we also must be absolutely trustworthy.

Eternity in Our Hearts

He hath set eternity in their heart.   Ecclesiastes 3:11

THE Preacher has been enumerating the various extremes and alternatives of existence. The natural conclusion might seem to be that since each neutralizes the other, it is just as well for a man to do nothing at all. But a deeper thought is suggested. Man is greater than the changes around him. He has eternity in his heart, and therefore all the varied circumstances of human life resemble the wheels of some great machine, the cogs of which turn in different directions, but the effect is a forward motion manufacturing a fabric that will outlive the machinery that made it.

We are greater than circumstance, or change, or things. We have the capacity for the Eternal and Infinite. As the sea-shell sighs for the ocean, so our hearts cry out, though sometimes inarticulately, for the living God. Christ said that foxes have holes and the birds their nests, but the Son of Man hath not where to lay his head; and this is true in another sense. The noblest men are those least able to rest anywhere short of God.

God made man in His own image; and nothing more surely attests the greatness of our origin than the faculties of our souls which are capable of yearning for, conceiving, and enjoying the Infinite, the Immortal, and the Divine.

Let us come to Him who has the words of eternal life, who is Himself the Bread that endures unto eternal life. He that comes to Him shall never hunger; he that believes in Him shall never thirst.

> Here would we end our quest;
>   Alone are found in Thee
> The life of perfect bliss — the rest
>   Of immortality.

He Waits to Be Gracious

*Therefore will the Lord wait, that he may be gracious unto you,
and therefore will he be exalted, that he may have mercy upon
you.* Isaiah 30:18

AS long as the people tried to help themselves, sending
ambassadors to Egypt and seeking an alliance against the in-
vader, God could do nothing for them. He could only wait
until they returned to simple reliance upon Himself. In returning to trust and rest they would be saved. At first they
refused. They were opposed to the idea of simple trust in
God. It seemed impossible to believe that if they simply
rested on Him, He would do better for them than their most
strenuous exertions could do. And all the while God was
waiting till every expedient failed, and they were reduced
to such a condition that He could step in and save them.

How like this is to much in our lives! It is long before
we learn the lesson of returning and rest; of quietness and
confidence. We will trust in chariots and horses, and ride
upon the swift. It is, of course, right to use the means God
has provided; but our strong temptation is to put them in
the place of God, and trust them.

*We are trying to save ourselves from the just penalty of
our sin,* from the pursuit of our foes, from perplexing com-
plications of circumstances; we have been running
backwards and forwards, flurried and excited. At how many
doors we have knocked to find them closed. And all the
while God has been waiting to be gracious to us; waiting
till we came to the end of ourselves; waiting, till like a spent
struggler in the water, we ceased from our frantic efforts
and cast ourselves back upon His strong everlasting love.
He can only save in one way — His way. Blessed are they
that wait for Him. The soul that waits for God will always
find the God for whom he waits.

For His Name's Sake

For mine own sake, for mine own sake, will I do it; for how should my name be profaned.   Isaiah 48:11

GOD finds His supreme motive in Himself. Mark how strongly He insists on it. "For my Name's sake will I defer mine anger; and for my praise will I refrain from thee." And in this verse He twice repeats, "for mine own sake." Surely this is a matter for extreme comfort and consolation.

If God had saved us because of some trait of natural beauty and attractiveness which He beheld in us, He might turn from us when it faded before the touch of years. The woman whose only claim on attention and homage is in her face — who has no other qualities to command and retain respect, must dread the inevitable effect of time. We would be, therefore, perpetually anxious if God's motive were only one of pity or complacency.

But God's motive is His character, His name and nature, the maintenance of His honor in the face of the universe. God is too deeply implicated in our salvation to show signs of variableness or the shadow of turning. He did not begin to save us because we were worthy or lovely, but because He would. Therefore He will not give up because we prove ourselves weak and worthless and difficult to save. There are times when we can only cast ourselves on His infinite grace and say, "Save me for Thine own Name's sake." And when we have been overcome by sin, it is good to go to Him and say, "Father, I have nothing to plead but Thy own nature and name declared in Jesus: for His sake, because Thou hast made a promise to Him, and to me in Him; for Thy glory's sake defer Thine anger, forgive my sins; save me for Thine own Name's sake."

The Iniquity of Us All

All we like sheep have gone astray; we have turned every one to his own way; and the Lord hath laid on him the iniquity of us all. Isaiah 53:6

THE Lord did it, because He was the Lord, and He took on Himself the iniquity of us all. All the evil of the world came together as though many confluent streams poured their poisonous substances into one foaming maelstrom which filled the heart of the dying Savior. The Apostle Peter well summarized it in the matchless sentence, "Who his own self bare our sins in his own body on the tree" (I Peter 2:24).

This verse begins and ends with all. We are all alike in having "gone astray." We have not all gone in the same direction, nor all to the same extent. We are not equally far from the fold. But we are all away from it. They say that if sheep can stray, they will; and there is no animal more hopeless and helpless than sheep which have escaped their pen. The ox knows his owner and his master's crib; the dog and cat will make their way home. But the sheep wanders on in small and ever smaller companies, until it is entrapped in the rocks, or devoured by wolves, or harried to death by dogs. Such were we. Panting, driven, chased, weary; but Jesus sought us, and brought us back to the fold, and gave us a name and place among His own.

But how can we forget the cost we have been to the Shepherd? See ye not the wounds in his hands and feet? Know ye not that His heart was lacerated and broken by the burden of our sins? "Our own way," that has been the curse of our lives, and the agony of our Shepherd. Would that it might be forever blocked against us, and that we might be led in His own way!

A Mother's Comfort

As one whom his mother comforteth, so will I comfort you.
Isaiah 66:13

THERE is the mother nature as well as that of the father in God. We are familiar with the thought of the divine Fatherhood; let us not forget the divine Motherhood. All the soft, gentle touches of mother's hand, unlike any other hands; all the tender pleading, yearning affection; all the utter selflessness, that never regards what it expends for the objects of its love, are equally in God. But as men get mad with drink and sin, and refuse the sweet mother-love which would gather them, until worn-out and weary they come back to it wrecked and forlorn, so we have drifted from God's mother-heart. Fools that we are!

Come back to it, children! Like wayward runaway babes, at the end of the long summer's day, who, shamefaced and sorrowful, with their torn clothes and grimy faces, hardly dare present themselves to those tender eyes. Yet they know they may count on the most tender reception. So come back to Him. He will receive, forgive, cleanse, comfort.

A mother's comfort! Estimate it at its full. Remember how your mother comforted you, as a little child; as a man at the death of your young wife; as a maiden when love had disappointed. How much more God! May we not then address to God's tender heart those most exquisite words:

Neither love me for
Thine own dear pity's wiping my cheeks dry,
Since one might well forget to weep who bore
Thy comfort long, and lose thy love thereby;
But love me for love's sake, that evermore
Thou mayst love on through love's eternity.

Walkways behind the Wailing Wall

Call Unto Me

Call unto me, and I will answer thee, and show thee great and mighty things.   Jeremiah 33:3

WE must learn the sacred art of prayer. God says, "Call unto Me." He likes us to address Him in prayer. We may believe that He will do His best, but this may degenerate into a subtle excuse for lethargy; and therefore God stirs us by the invitation to call upon Him. There is no assurance that He will show us these great and mighty things, unless we obey the injunction of our text to call on Him. But we must, as did the disciples, ask the Lord to teach us to pray. The prayer which is born of God, rises to God from whom it came with the certainty of an answer.

God seeks intercessors. He longs to dispense larger blessings. He longs to reveal His power and glory as God, His saving grace, His comfort and peace. But He is limited by the smallness and fewness of our prayers. He cannot do what He would for the Church in the world, because of our unbelief. He cries to us "Call unto Me." Little prayer, little blessing; more prayer, more blessing; much prayer, much blessing.

But what a promise is here. We long to see great things done for God in our churches and missions, in the hearts and lives of our friends. We long to see the difficult things unknotted, so that the crooked are made straight, and the rough smooth. But all these things shall be. The impossibilities of our life are possible to God. The mysteries of our life yield their secrets at the summons of God. The iron gates shall open, the sea divide. Only get right with God; only let God have unhindered way through our life; only dare to believe that God answers prayer, and go forward in faith.

Shepherd of Our Souls

*I will feed my flock, and I will cause them to lie down, saith
the Lord God.* Ezekiel 34:15

IT is impossible to make sheep lie down unless they are
satisfied or free from alarm. Flocks lie deep in the rich
pasture lands only when they have eaten to the full, and are
quiet from fear of evil. When, therefore, the Shepherd and
Bishop of our souls promises that He will cause us to lie
down, He undertakes to fulfill in our life these two
conditions.

The Lord Jesus brings us into a good pasture, and causes
us to feed upon the mountains of fellowship, transfiguration,
and far-reaching vision. Listen as He cries, "Eat, yea, eat
abundantly, O beloved." Our restlessness arises from our
refusal to obey His loving invitation to come and dine. We
do not read our Bibles enough, or feed on His flesh, or
drink His blood. Let us look at the Scriptures as the green
pastures; and as we open them let us ask Him to be our
guide, and to show us the food appropriate to our need.

The Lord Jesus does more. He makes with us a covenant
of peace; and even if the evil beasts do not leave the land,
He assures us that we can dwell safely in the wilderness and
sleep in the woods. He intends that we should be safe in
Immanuel's land; that the bonds of our yoke should be
broken; and that we should be delivered out of the hands
of those who prey upon us.

*O child of God, be less dependent on people and cir-
cumstances!* Deal more constantly at first hand with Jesus.
Regard Him as our Shepherd; "He maketh to lie down." Rejoice that He the Lord our God is with us, and that the
shadowing woods, the mighty mountains, and the stream-
watered vales are equally beneath His power and care.

Fear Not

O man greatly beloved, fear not; peace be unto thee, be strong, yea, be strong.   Daniel 10:19

WHY should we fear? We are loved, greatly beloved; loved to God's uttermost; loved to the gift of His Only-begotten; loved to blood-shedding and death. It is said that Jesus, having loved His own, which were in the world, loved them unto the end; not to the end of His human ministry, but to the uttermost of what love can be.

Why should we fear? Has God done so much, and will He not do all? Has He brought us out of Egypt to let us perish in the wilderness? Is He so careful of the soul, and so careless of all beside? There are mysteries — mysteries of life and death, of sin and sorrow, of this world and the next. But fear not; God is ours, and we are His by immutable and indissoluble ties.

Let us possess ourselves in peace. We cannot understand, but we can trust. We may not know the way we are going, but we can lean back on the heart of our Guide. Standing in the cleft of the Rock, we can look out in peace on dreaded evils as they pass beyond our sight. If only we are acquainted with God, we shall be at peace, and thereby good will come to us. They fear who look at circumstances, and not in God's face.

And we shall be strong — strong to endure; strong to achieve; strong to wait; strong to carry the battle to the gate; strong to set our face like a flint, when the hour strikes for us to go to the cross; strong when called to follow the dear Master, Christ.

Be strong to hope, O heart! Though day is bright,
The stars can only shine in the dark night.
Be strong, O heart of mine, and look towards the light.

The Comfort of Immortality

*O death, where are thy plagues? O grave, where is thy
destruction? Hosea 13:14*

THESE words are made familiar to us in the magnificent
assurance at the close of Paul's great resurrection chapter —
I Corinthians 15. They have been recited for centuries over
Christian graves.

*In their first utterance they record Jehovah's resolve to
deliver His people in spite of all their sins.* The conflict in
God's heart between His hatred of idolatry and His ancient,
unalterable love, gives this chapter its remarkably disjointed
character. There is hardly a paragraph which is not marked by abrupt transitions, agitation of speech, appeals, in-
quiries, expressions of infinite regret. But notwithstanding
all, God has given commandment to bless, and He neither
could nor would reverse it. Let death and Hades do their
worst against His chosen, God was stronger still.

*In these last days these words may be quoted over every
Christian's death,* whether it be a martyrdom or the quiet
yielding up of life. In comparison with the great gain that
death brings to those who pass to the "far better" of being
with Christ, wherein are we losers by it?

*But the full realization of these words awaits the hour
when this corruptible shall put on incorruption,* and this
mortal shall put on immortality, at the sudden appearance
of the Savior in His advent glory. Then shall be brought to
pass the saying which is written, "Death is swallowed up
in victory." Not a soul shall be left behind. Not one of the
redeemed shall remain in the prison-house. Both the dead
and the living shall be caught up to meet the Lord in the
air, and shall ever be with Him (I Thessalonians 4:16,17).
This is our comfort.

What He Requires

What doth the Lord require of thee, but to do justly, love mercy, and walk humbly with thy God?   Micah 6:8

THE perfunctory sacrifices of lambs and rams, rivers of oil, and of tender children, were eagerly practiced by the surrounding nations, but were abhorrent to God. What to Him is the outward rite without the holy purpose; the child's form of obedience, apart from genuine love? It appears that the questions of this chapter were put by Balaam; and the words before us were uttered by the Divine Spirit to his heart. But however they may be, it is a matter for our adoring gratitude that God has stepped out of the infinite to show us what is good, and what He requires.

To do justly is to preserve the balance of strict equity: if an employer, treating workers with perfect justice; if a manufacturer or salesman, making and selling what will thoroughly satisfy the just requirements of the purchaser; if an employee, giving an exact equivalent of time and diligence and conscientious labor for money received.

To love mercy is to take into consideration all those drawbacks which misfortunes, which enfeebled health, or crushing sorrow may impose on those who owe us service or money.

To walk humbly with God implies constant prayer and watchfulness, familiar yet humble conversation, conscientious service, allowing nothing to divert us from His side. We must exchange our monologue, in which we talk with ourselves, for dialogue, in which we talk as we walk with God. Ask Him to make these good things the ordinary tenor of your life. For they are the answer to the question in the text, "What doth the Lord require of thee?"

The Mission of Immanuel

And she shall bring forth a son, and thou shalt call his name
Jesus, for he shall save his people from their sins.   Matthew 1:21

THIS is the mission of Immanuel. He came, not as the Jews expected, to break the yoke of Caesar and re-establish the kingdom of David; but to break the yoke of sin, and set up the kingdom of God. The Church has too often misunderstood the purpose of His coming, as though He meant simply to save from the consequences and results of sin. This was too limited a program for the Son of God. To cancel the results and leave the ⟐itter cause; to deliver from the penalty, but not from the power, to rescue His people from the grasp of a broken law, but confess Himself unable to deal with the bad virus of the blood — this was to fail. No; dare to take this announcement in its full and glorious meaning, written as it is.

What a mixture of blood flowed through His veins! Let our eyes glance through the list of His genealogy. Men and women, notorious for their evil character, lie in the direct line of His descent. This was permitted, that He might fully represent our fallen race; that no sinner, however bad, should be ashamed to claim His help; and that it should be clearly shown how powerless sin was to tarnish or taint the holiness of His sinless nature. Made in the likeness of sinful flesh, He knew no sin. The germs of corruption could find no welcome in His heart.

Art thou one of His people? Hast thou accepted His rule, and allied thyself with Him? For if so, He shall save thee. Though possessed with sins throughout, He will blot them out.

The Jordan River

Covenant and Communion

For this is my blood of the covenant, which is poured out for many unto remission of sins. Matthew 26:28

THE first covenant was not ratified without blood. For when every commandment had been spoken by Moses, he took the blood of the calves and goats, sprinkled the people, and said, "This is the blood of the covenant" (Hebrews 9:19,20). So the second covenant must be ratified by blood; not by that of calves and goats, but by the precious blood of Jesus Himself. He who made the covenant sealed it with His blood, that we might have strong assurance.

But Christ has put the cup which holds the emblem of His blood into our hands, and bids us drink it. What, then, do we mean when at the Supper we lift that sacred cup to our lips? Are we not saying by that significant act, remember Thy covenant? Are we not reminding Jesus that we are relying upon Him to do His part? Are we not pledging ourselves to Him as His own, bound to Him by indissoluble ties, and satisfied with His most blessed service?

Among the most precious promises of the new covenant is that God promises to remember our sins no more. Here is the ground which enables God to forgive so freely. The blood has been shed for many unto the remission of sins; the claims of infinite justice have been met; the righteous demands of a broken law satisfied; the barriers have been removed that might have restrained the manifestation of divine love. And now we may sit with Christ at His table in His kingdom, not as rebels, but as welcome guests.

Why Trouble the Master Now?

While he yet spake, they came from the ruler of the synagogue's house, saying, Thy daughter is dead: why troublest thou the Master any further? Mark 5:35

WHAT hopelessness! They had watched the sweet flower fade, till no color was left on the pale cheek, and the merry voice was still; and then they thought of the Galilean Teacher. "Why cost Him time and trouble? His visit will be useless now! It was very kind of Him to be willing to come! But it is now of no use! Very kind; but no use." Their limited faith deceived them.

We go to God in comparatively small trials, and think He can help us. But there are times when we say, "It is no use troubling further; we must just bear our trial as well as we can, for it would be improper to trouble God with it any more. But what tires us does not tire the tireless Lord, and what is a bother to us is no bother to Him at all. The great mistake of humanity is found in Psalms 50:21: "Thou thoughtest that I was altogether such a one as thyself."

But Jesus knows the way out. He says in His sweet undertone, "Fear not! only believe." He has the keys of death. He never would have let things come to this awful pass by His delay unless He had known that, even if the worse came to the worst, all would end well. He has purposely delayed that He might show you what God can do. Fear not! The hand of the Almighty Savior has yours within its grasp. He will not let you stumble as you go down this dark staircase by His side. Only believe; have faith in Him.

Can We Believe?

*If thou canst do anything, have compassion on us, and help us.
And Jesus said unto him, If thou canst!*   Mark 9:22,23

YES, there was an *if* in this sad case. But the father put it in the wrong place. He put it against Christ's power, "If Thou canst do anything." But it was really on the side of his own ability to believe. If only he believed, all else would be easily possible. Even though his faith were small, it would suffice. The tiniest seed can appropriate the chemical products of the soil, and transmute them into digestible products; the narrowest channel can carry the waters of the whole ocean, if you give time enough. Let us not worry as much about the greatness or smallness of our faith, but whether it is directed towards the living Savior.

There are many issues to which these words may be applied. If Jesus can save me from the power of sin! No; if we can believe, He can. If Jesus can deliver out of a mesh of temptation and perplexity! No; if we can believe, He will. If Jesus can revive His work mightily to the upbuilding of His Church and the ingathering of the lost! No; if we can believe, He can.

Do you want that kind of faith? It can be yours. Look away from difficulty and temptation to Jesus; consider Him; familiarize yourself with the promises; study what He has done for others — and you will believe.

> All things are possible to God,
>   To Christ the power of God in man
> To me, when I am all subdued,
>   When I in Christ am formed again,
> And witness from my sins set free,
>   All things are possible to me.

His Darkest Hour

My God, my God, why hast thou forsaken me?   Mark 15:34

THIS was the darkest hour of the Savior's human life.
Lover and friend stood away from Him; and those for
whom His blood was being shed covered Him with con-
tempt and abuse. Let us consider:

His quotation of scripture. He is quoting the first verse
of Psalm 22, which is truly known as the Psalm of the
Cross. He may have recited to Himself that wonderful
lamentation, in which David was to anticipate so minutely
the sufferings of his Lord. What meaning there was for those
dying lips in the 7th verse: "All they that see me laugh me
to scorn"; in the 13th: "They gape upon me"; in the 14th:
"All my bones are out of joint"; or in the 18th: "They part
my garments and cast lots." What sacred feet trod those
well-worn steps!

His vicarious sufferings. There is no possible way of
understanding or interpreting these words, except by believing that He was suffering for sins not His own; that He was
being made sin for us; that He was bearing away the sin
of the world. It is not for a moment conceivable that the
Father could have ever seemed to forsake His well-beloved
Son, unless He stood as the representative of a guilty race,
and during those hours of midday midnight became the pro-
pitiation for the sins of the world.

His perfect example of the way of faith. In doing the
Father's will, He yielded up His life even to the death of the
cross. But amid it all He said, "My God, my God." He still
held to the Father with His two hands. And His faith con-
quered. The clouds broke; the clear heaven appeared; He
died with a serene faith. "My God" was exchanged for
"Father, into thy hands I commend my spirit" (Luke 23:46).

Glory and Peace

Glory to God in the highest, and on earth peace among men.
Luke 2:14

THESE two magnificent attributes are joined together, and none can separate them. Do you want peace? Your highest aim must be the glory of God. Do you seek God's glory as your highest aim? Then, the inevitable result will be the peace that passeth understanding.

Glory to God in the highest. It was said of the soldiers of the first Napoleon, that they were content to die in the ditch if only he rode over them to victory. With their last breath they cried, "Long live the Emperor!" It seemed as though they had lost all thought and care of their own interests, so long as glory accrued to his name. So should it be of us. Higher than our own comfort, or success, or popularity, should be the one thought of the glory of our God. Let Christ be honored, loved, exalted, at whatever cost to us.

On earth, peace. It will come, because when the heart has only one aim to follow, it is delivered from dividing and distracting cares. It will come, because the glory of God is so lofty an aim that it lifts the soul into the atmosphere of the heavenly and eternal world, where peace reigns unbroken. It will come, because we are not greatly troubled by the reverses and set-backs common to all work in this world, since the main object is always secure and beyond fear of failure. Though the waves ebb and flow, the tide is coming up and will soon stand at high-water mark.

This peace will come only to those in whom God is well pleased. Live to please God, and He will breathe on thee His peace. Seek His glory, and He will make thy heart His home. Do His will, and thereby good shall come to thee.

The Elder Brother

But he was angry, and would not go in.   Luke 15:28

THE elder brother is the dark contrast which heightens the glowing picture of the repentant prodigal, as the gargoyle does the beauty of the angel faces on the cathedral wall.

When we look at sin, not in its theological aspects, but in its everyday clothes, we find that it comes in two kinds. We find that there are sins of the body and sins of the disposition; or, more narrowly, sins of the passions (including all forms of lust and selfishness) and sins of the temper. The prodigal is the instance in the New Testament of sins of passion — the elder brother of sins of temper.

Now we might be disposed to think that the prodigal is the worse sinner of these two; but it is interesting to note that as the story ends, we see him found, forgiven, restored; while the elder brother is still outside the house, absent from the feast. Does Christ mean that the ill-tempered murmuring of the Pharisee is more hopeless than the passion of the publican and sinner? We must not press the thought too far. But we may at least ask if we are harboring, beneath a very respectable, moral exterior the spirit of the elder brother, who plods daily to work, and is accounted a paragon of virtue, but cannot celebrate the return of a brother.

If we made a careful analysis of the ingredients of that one spiteful speech, they come out thus: jealousy, anger, pride, lack of love, cruelty, self-righteousness, sulkiness, touchiness, stubbornness. His speech, like a bubble escaping to the surface of the pool, betrays the rottenness beneath. Let us carefully read our hearts, lest there be any trace of this spirit in ourselves, when others are pressing into the kingdom with joy.

Sifted as Wheat

Simon, Simon, behold Satan asked to have you that he might sift you as wheat. Luke 22:31

THE Master apparently did not pray that temptation should be withheld. The quick eye of His affection had discerned the tempter's approach. His quick ear had detected Satan's request of the Father; as though he said, "Let me have the chance for one brief hour, and I will show that these men, so far from being gold, silver, and precious stones, are only wood, hay, and stubble." But though He knew all this, the Master did not request that the winnowing wind should be withheld. Why?

Because temptation is part of the present order of the world. Why it is so we cannot tell; that it is so we know assuredly. Why the Almighty permitted the Evil One to intrude and to assail every single soul of woman born, we shall probably never understand until mystery drops from our eyes in the glistening light of heaven. We only are sure that the permission of temptation is not inconsistent with His almightiness or goodness.

Because temptation tests character and reveals us to ourselves and to one another. Was it not better that Peter should know how weak he was; that he might become truly penitent and converted? Was it not befitting that Judas should be exposed before the Day of Pentecost? Was it not best that the foundation stones of the Church should be well tested? Is it not better to learn our weakness now and here than at the Judgment?

Threshing grain

We Shall See

*Because I saw thee under the fig tree, believest thou? Thou shalt
see greater things than these.* John 1:50

GOD deals with us always on an ascending scale. If we
see clearly the lowest rung in the heavenly ladder, while we
behold, the vail of mist will part, and we shall see the next
above it, and in due order, the next. And so the steps that
slope away through darkness up to God will always beckon
us to greater and yet greater things.

Have you known Christ as the Word? He is more; both
Spirit and Life.

Has He become flesh? You shall behold Him glorified with
the glory He had before the worlds.

Have you known Him as Alpha, before all? He is also
Omega.

Do you know the baptism by water? You shall be bap-
tized by fire.

Have you beheld the Lamb on the Cross? You shall
behold Him in the midst of the throne.

Have you followed Christ to His tomb carved in the
hillside? You shall enter with Him into mansions of eternal
glory.

Do you acknowledge Him as King of Israel? You shall
hear the acclamations that salute Him as King of the worlds.

Live up to all you know, and you shall know more. Be
all you can, and you shall become more. Do all that your
talents permit, and you will find yourself ruler over many
cities.

74

The Gift of God

Jesus said unto her, if thou knewest the gift of God thou wouldest have asked of him, and he would have given thee living water. John 4:10

THERE are wonderful contrasts here. He who gives rest sits weary on the wellhead. He who was the Jews' Messiah utters His deepest lessons to a woman of Samaria. He that gives living water asks for water from the dark, cool depths that lay beneath them.

God's best things are gifts. Light, air, natural beauty, the sense of vigorous health, human love, and above all, His only begotten and beloved Son. Among all other gifts can any compare to this? The living spring of eternal life is an altogether unspeakable gift — nothing can purchase it. Our attempts to give all our resources in an effort to buy it would be utterly useless. It must be received as a gift, or not at all.

God's gifts must be asked for. "Thou wouldest have asked, and He would have given." This is the law of Heaven. Prayer is a necessary link between the Divine Hand that gives and the human heart that receives. We have not, because we ask not. There is nothing in our Lord's words of the dreamy and weak pietism which refuses to ask because it will not dictate to the perfect wisdom of God.

If we had fuller knowledge we would pray more. "If thou knewest . . . thou wouldest ask." If we knew who He is that stands beside us in the hours of private prayer — if we knew all the possibilities of the life of prayer — if we knew what gains would come to us on our knees, we would give ourselves to prayer, as though it were the main object of our lives.

Believing Is Seeing

Let not your heart be troubled: ye believe in God, believe also in me. John 14:1

IF WE were less familiar with these words, we would be more startled by their immeasurable meaning. One who seems a man asks all men to give Him precisely the same faith and confidence they give to God. Though He was the humblest and meekest of men, He continued His appeal. And the irresistible conclusion is forced on us, that He was and knew Himself to be "God manifest in the flesh."

Faith in Jesus is the cure of heart trouble. It is of little use to say, "Let not your heart be troubled," unless you can add "Trust Christ." Only if we can trust can we be still. Only if we can shift the responsiblity of our life on the care of our never-failing Redeemer can weeping be exchanged for radiant and unspeakable joy.

Faith in Jesus produces knowledge of God. "Believe Me that I am in the Father, and the Father in Me." Philip said, "Show us the Father." Jesus answered, "Believe, and thou dost behold." The world says, "Seeing is believing." Jesus says, "Believing is seeing." The true way to know God is, not by arguing about or seeking to verify His existence by intellectual processes, but by obeying the precepts of Jesus; following the footsteps of Jesus; holding fellowship with Jesus.

Faith in Jesus makes our lives channels through which He can work. "He that believeth on me, the works . . ." (verses 12-14). The Gospels are included in the one clause; the Acts and all the marvels of the following ages in the other. Jesus is always the worker; and the one who yields himself most utterly to Him in obedience and faith, will become the channel through which He will work most mightily.

Not of This World

Jesus answered, my kingdom is not of this world.   John 18:36.

WELL might Pilate question if Jesus was really a king. A poor, weary, despised Nazarene, rejected by the very ones to whom He was sent. A strange contrast, surely, to the King Herod who built those halls of judgment! But Jesus did not abate His claims, "Thou sayest that I am a king." And as the ages have passed they have substantiated His claim.

The origin of His kingdom. "My kingdom is not of this world." The Lord did not mean, as His words have been too often interpreted, that His kingdom had nothing to do with this world; but that it did not originate here. The "of" means "from." Jesus is King, not by earthly descent or human right, but by the purpose and counsel of the Father, who said, "Thou art my Son; this day have I begotten Thee: yet will I set my King upon my holy hill of Zion."

The method of its advancement. It is not spread by armed force. His servants fight a spiritual warfare. They are priests clad in the white robes of immaculate purity, bearing aloft their banner with the inscription, "Blessed are the peacemakers." Like their Master, they bear witness to the truth; and as they do so those who are of the truth are attracted to the Lord, as steel filings to a magnet.

There is true royalty in bearing witness to the truth. Humbly we may appropriate our Master's words: to this end were we born, and for this cause are we left in the world, that in every act and word we might bear witness to the Truth. As we do so, we manifest a royalty which is not of human gift or descent, but which has been communicated by the reception of the Christ through the regenerating power of His word.

The Eyes of Love

That disciple therefore whom Jesus loved saith unto Peter, It is the Lord. John 21:7

THIS miracle was also a parable. When we go fishing without Jesus, we may indeed toil all night and take nothing. But when through the darkness Jesus comes, and speaks to us across the waves, and tells us where to let down the nets; when we are in blessed partnership with Him; when, though we see Him not, we obey His slightest promptings — then our nets are filled to their uttermost.

Those who are loved, love. It was the consciousness that Jesus loved him which made John "the Apostle of Love." Love casts such a wondrous spell over its objects, that they begin to shine in its rays and reflect them. Nothing will make a coal glow with heat but to plunge it into the heart of the fire. Do you want to love the Lord Jesus? Then dwell on His love for you.

Those who love Christ see Him. It was not Peter, the man of eager action, but John, the man of devoted love, that saw the Master amid the haze that lay on the lake shore. Love will penetrate every disguise; will detect Him by the slightest sign; will strip from our eyes the film of sin drawn over them. If we loved Him more, we would see His hand even in that disappointment, that crushing sorrow.

Those who seek Christ cannot keep it to themselves. They must tell it to their companions, with beating heart and thrilling speech. John said unto Peter, "It is the Lord." Is not this what we may all experience as we draw near to eternity? Shall we not see Jesus standing on the shore, with preparations beyond all thought, to welcome us as we arrive from the night cruise?

Giving Ourselves to Prayer

Look ye out among you seven men whom we may appoint over this business. But we will give ourselves continually to prayer. Acts 6:3,4

IF ever there was a sacred work, it was caring for these poor widows; and yet the apostles felt that even such duties might interfere with the continual ministry of intercession. No doubt they always lived in the atmosphere and spirit of prayer, but they rightly felt that this was not enough either for them or their work. So they sought a division of labor, that while some specifically served tables and ministered the funds of the church, others would be free to continue steadfastly in prayer. This would keep the communication with the King on the throne clear and fresh, would draw down the power and blessing of the heavenly world, securing wisdom and strength for their great responsibilities.

There are many courses of usefulness open to each of us in this world, and we must choose the one, not only most suited to our talents, but in which we can best serve our day and generation. It may be that in our incessant activities, we neglect the one method by which we may contribute the most to the furtherance of our Father's kingdom. Notice that word "give." It is as though the Spirit of prayer were seeking natures so pure, so devoted, that without hindrance He might form Himself into them. Give yourself to Him for this!

"In that day," said our Lord, speaking of the Day of Pentecost, *"ye shall ask in my name."* It is only when we are full of the spirit of prayer that we can experience the true power to plead with God, and use the name of Christ effectively to receive His richest blessings. Much prayer, much blessing; little prayer, little blessing; no prayer, no blessing.

The Justifier

That he might be just and the justifier of him that hath faith in Jesus. Romans 3:26

THIS verse is often quoted as though the word *yet* must be inserted to bring out its meaning. "Just, and yet the Justifier." This adds emphasis to the marvel of a just God justifying sinful men. Of course, this is a true thought and marvelous. But it is not the precise ideal of the Apostle, when he says that the just God is the Justifier of those that have faith in Jesus. He means that the very justice of God has come on our side, and that His love may have its unhindered way, not only consistently with His justice, but because of it.

This is the heart of the Gospel. Jesus has stood as our representative. He has borne our sin, in its curse and penalty; has met the claims of a broken law, and satisfied the demands of infinite righteousness. To have done this in our name and on our behalf not only makes us free from any penalty which might otherwise have accrued, but gives us a claim — the claim of the righteous — on all those blessings which the righteous God has to bestow.

As we become one with Jesus by a living faith, we stand possessed of all that He has done and is. In Him we have already suffered all that the holy law of God could demand as the just penalty of our sins. In Him we have lain in the grave, paying the uttermost price that could be exacted. In Him we have been liberated from the prison, and have passed into the presence and welcome of God. We are saved not only by the grace, but by the justice of God. He is faithful to his Son and just to the law, when He forgives us our sins.

He Staggered Not

*He staggered not at the promise of God through unbelief; but
was strong in faith, giving glory to God.* Romans 4:20

IT was a marvelous promise that this childless pair should
have a child, and become progenitors of a great nation, so
that the stars of the heavenly spaces and the sand grains on
the ocean shore should not be more numerous. The promise
was enough to stagger any man, but Abraham staggered
not. How was this?

*His unstaggering faith did not come from ignoring the dif-
ficulties.* He might have done so. Whenever the natural
obstacles arose in his mind, he might have ignored them.
But this was not Abraham's policy. He quietly and
deliberately considered the enormous difficulties that lay in
the path of the divine purpose, and in spite of them "he
staggered not."

*His unstaggering faith arose from his great thoughts of
him who had promised.* He kept saying to himself, "He is
able, He is able." He knew that God would not have promised what He could not perform. He knew that the God of
nature was also Lord of the nature He had made. He knew
that no word of the Almighty could be destitute of power.
He fed his faith by cherishing lofty and profound thoughts
of God's infinite resources. There rang in his heart the
assurance, "I am El Shaddai."

It is remarkable that throughout Abraham's life, God was
continually giving him new glimpses into His own glorious
nature. With every temptation, call to obedience, or demand
for sacrifice, a new and deeper revelation was entwined.
This fed his faith, and gave it unstaggering strength. Child
of God, feed your faith on Promise. For every look at your
difficulties, take ten at the power of our God.

Fishermen on the Sea of Galilee

Partners with Christ

God is faithful by whom ye were called unto the fellowship of his Son Jesus Christ our Lord. I Corinthians 1:9

THE word for fellowship is the same that is employed in Luke 5:10, of James and John being partners with Peter. We are privileged to have been called into partnership with the Son of God, in His redemptive purposes, His love and tears for men, and ultimately in His triumph and glory. In the words of the Apostle, "our fellowship (or partnership) is with the Father, and with his Son Jesus Christ our Lord."

How comforting is the thought that Christ's interests are ours, and that we are at liberty to draw upon His resources to the uttermost. Suppose a poor clerk for a wealthy company is summoned from his desk into the office of the president, and informed that he has been taken into partnership with the firm. Would it not be less of an honor than has been bestowed on us? Association with millionaires in money-making is infinitely less desirable than association with the Son of God in world-saving. And would that poor clerk feel any anxiety as to his share in meeting the immense liabilities of the concern? However great they might be, he would know that the resources of the firm were adequate, and he would be able to sleep easily at night, though millions were due on the morrow. Child of God, cannot our Father meet all His Son's engagements?

The call to this partnership is from the Father. It is He who has chosen us for this high honor of cooperating with His Son. Will He lead us into such an association, and then leave us to be overwhelmed by the difficulties of the situation He has created? It cannot be! He will supply all our need.

The Greatest

The greatest of these is love. I Corinthians 13:13

WHAT a thrilling expression must have shone on the Apostle's face, the face of one who knew God and who knew love, as he broke into this exquisite tribute, this perfect poem of love! Why is love the greatest?

Because it is the crown of the other two, and includes them. Faith is the root; hope is the stem; love the perfect flower. You may have faith without hope, and hope without love, but you cannot have love apart from faith and hope.

Because it is most like God. God's nature is not especially characterized by faith, because there is no uncertainty with His perfect knowledge; nor by hope, because there is no future to His eternal existence. But God is love; and to love is to resemble Him.

Because it will immeasurably outlast the other two. Human knowledge is only at best the spellings of babes, and will vanish in the perfect light of heaven. Eloquence will seem like the lispings of infancy. Prophecies will have no place, because all the landscape of the future will be revealed. Faith and hope will be lost in realization, but love only will last forever.

Because love brings the purest rapture. "What is heaven?" asked a wealthy Christian of his minister. "I will tell you what it is," was the quick reply. "If you will go to the store, and buy provisions and goods, and take them to that poor widow on the hillside, who has three of her children sick. She is poor, and a member of the Church. Take a nurse, and someone to cook the food. When you get there, read the Twenty-third Psalm, and kneel by her side and pray. Then you will find out in part what heaven is."

Seeing the Unseen

While we look not at the things which are seen, but at the things which are not seen: for the things which are seen are temporal; but the things which are not seen are eternal. II Corinthians 4:18

WE are here encouraged to look through the things which are seen; to consider them as the glass window through which we pass to that which is behind and beyond. You do not waste your time by admiring the frame or setting of some rare jewel, but penetrate to the jewel itself. So, day by day, look through the material and transient to the eternal purpose, the divine idea, the deep that lieth under.

Look for God's thought in all the incidents, circumstances, and objects of your daily life. Do not stop at the outward; penetrate to the inward and eternal. Beneath that bitter physical suffering there are stores of divine fortitude and grace. Beneath that trying circumstance there are celestial compensations. Beneath those sweet family ties there are suggestions of love and friendship, which can never grow old or pass away. Beneath the letter of Scripture is the spirit; beneath the ordinance, oneness with the loving Savior.

When this is the attitude of our soul, afflictions that might otherwise have weighed heavy, become light; and those that drag through long and tedious years, will seem but for a moment. And without exception, the light and momentary afflictions will produce the quality of character that can contain the far more exceeding and eternal weight of glory.

Abound in This Also

See that ye abound in this grace also. II Corinthians 8:7-9

THE grace of liberality is as much a gift of God as faith, or utterance, or knowledge, or love. The Apostle Paul says that he desires to make known the grace of God, which had been given to the churches of Macedonia, so that they were able in their deep poverty to abound in riches of liberality.

This grace first dwelt in our blessed Lord, who, though He was rich, for our sakes became poor, that we through His poverty might become rich. If yours is a grudging disposition, be sure to appropriate the royal nature of the Lord Jesus, that it may fill and possess you.

Probably there is no greater test of our true religion than our behavior in giving. How few, comparatively, give in proportion to their income! How few give systematically! How few have learned the joy and luxury of giving, so that they abound therein!

This arises partly because we do not realize that we are stewards of God's property, and that He expects us to devote all we own to Him, keeping back only a necessary percentage for ourselves and our families, as a steward might who was farming an estate for his absent master. And partly it arises from mistrust of God, and the fear that some day there may be a sudden shortage of supplies. Oh that each of us would consider that all is God's, and begin by always giving a certain proportion of our earnings, so as not to rob God of His own. Pray day and night that we may abound in this grace also. Then, in faith that God is answering our prayer, let us begin to conquer our miserly, stingy character. Even though it protest — Give!

Strength in Weakness

When I am weak, then am I strong. II Corinthians 12:10

WE need not discuss the nature of Paul's thorn in the flesh. It is enough that he calls it "a stake," as though he had been impaled. It must have, therefore, been very painful. It must also have been physical, because he could not have prayed thrice for the removal of a moral taint, and been refused. It came from Satan, permitted by God, as in the case of Job, to buffet His servant. It is likely that he suffered from weak eyes, or some distressing eye disease; hence the eagerness of the Galatian converts to give him their eyes (Galatians 4:15).

God does not take away our thorns, but He communicates sufficient grace. He always answers prayer, though not as we expect. Let the music of these tender words soar unto thee, poor sufferer! "My grace is sufficient even for thee." Sufficient when friends forsake, and foes pursue; sufficient to make you strong against an infuriated crowd and a tyrannical judge; sufficient for excessive physical exertion and spiritual conflict; sufficient to enable you to do as much work, and even more, than if health and vigor were not impaired, because the very weakness of our nature is the chosen condition in which God will manifest the strength of His.

Do not bend under that mistaken marriage, that uncongenial business, that physical weakness, as though your life must be a failure; but take in large reinforcements of that divine grace which is given to the weak and to those who have no might. Paul clearly had reached such a condition, that he felt blessed to be deficient in much that men hold dear, and to have what most men dread. He rejoiced in all that diminished his personal power and strengthened his hold on God.

God's Poetry

We are his workmanship, created in Christ Jesus unto good works. Ephesians 2:10

THE Greek word might be literally rendered "poem." We are God's poem to the world — God's poetry. As the meter varies in the poems of a poet, so does the course of one life differ from another; but God has a thought, a plan, a purpose for each.

Created for good works. How carefully the Apostle defines the true position of works in the divine life. In the foregoing verses he insists that we are not saved by our works, that none should boast. But, to meet the objection that his system was inconsistent with holy living, he affirms that the whole intention of God was that we should manifest our new life in Christ by the fruit of a holy life. We were created in Him unto good works. Whatever good works may be demanded of you, dare to believe that you were created in Christ Jesus to do them. There is a perfect adjustment between the two.

The good works prepared. God who made us has prepared an ideal path for us. We may not follow it, but God has a perfect plan for our life. It may lie up hill or down; may be lined with grassy fields or full of jagged stones; may be short with the years of childhood or long with those of old age — but every path has been prepared.

Our daily walk. We do not have to make our own path, unless we chose to rebel against God; we may simply follow the path of God, one step at a time. And when the heart or flesh fails, when the way seems too difficult, or the door too strait — we must look always unto Jesus, who has gone along the same track, asking that His righteousness may go before us, and set us in the way of His steps (Psalm 85:13).

A Family Likeness

Be ye therefore imitators of God, as beloved children.
Ephesians 5:1

CHILDREN usually resemble their father or mother. There is often an unmistakable family likeness, which compels the most casual observer to exlaim, "The very image of his father." Oh that in each of us there might be that which would make men think of God!

Put away your former manner of life (4:22). The old man stands for the collection of habits, sayings, and doings which characterized our unregenerate days. The Apostle says that they are to be put away suddenly, instantly. Evidently this is possible, or such a command would not be issued. We speak of a gradual reformation, and advise the piecemeal discontinuance of evil. God, on the contrary, bids us treat the evil past like a company of soldiers would treat bandits and outlaws.

Be renewed in the spirit of your mind (4:23). We are reminded of Romans 12:2. The mind needs to be brought into daily, hourly contact with God's thoughts, as contained in Scripture, that it may be renewed. Otherwise, our constant association with the men and women of the world, their maxims and practices, will inevitably and sorrowfully deteriorate our thoughts. The only source of daily renewal is fellowship with God.

Put on the new man. The Apostle affirms that the new man is of God and was created by God when our Lord rose from the dead. The day of resurrection was one of creation. All the habits and dispositions of a holy, godlike life have been prepared for us in Him, and await our appropriation. Therefore, as we put on the new man, we shall become imitators of God as dear children.

That We May Be Holy

As therefore ye received Christ Jesus the Lord, so walk in him. Colossians 2:6

WHEN we were first brought to Jesus, we received Him into our hearts by faith. Throwing open the door, we bade Him welcome; and He came in. Though He was as unseen as the wind, and silent as light, He came. And there was a perfume as of myrrh, aloes, and cassia; like that which fills the ivory palaces of eternity.

Now the Apostle says that all our Christian life is to be lived on the same principle. The holy life is an attitude. Holiness is not an attainment of which we may boast, but an openness of soul towards the Lord Jesus, like a window unshuttered and uncurtained to the light. The believer is never independent of Jesus; but at every moment we are receiving from His fulness grace upon grace. We do not receive His qualities and attributes as things apart from the Lord Jesus; but receiving Him, we obtain them. The holy man is he who has learned the art of receiving Jesus; the holier, who has a greater capacity, through humility and faith; the holiest, he who can receive most of the life of the Son of God.

Our daily life is here compared to a walk. If we want to remain in Christ, there is no alternative but to take what God has marked out for you; though you may choose your atmosphere or environment. Every step may be taken in Christ; rooted in Him as a tree in rich soil; builded up as a house on a rock; inhaling His very breath as the life of life. And whatever the need may be, there is always an abundant supply in the Lord Jesus, in whom all treasures are hid. He teaches us that we may know; He indwells that we may be.

Olive tree in the Garden of Gethsemane

A Quiet Sanctification

The God of peace himself sanctify you wholly; and may your spirit and soul and body be preserved entire, without blame at the coming of our Lord.   I Thessalonians 5:23

OUR God has set Himself to the work of our sanctification. He looks upon us as His inheritance, and He will not rest until He has brought every acre of territory under cultivation. It is not enough that briars and thistles should be exterminated; they must be replaced by the rare growth of Christian virtue, which is Christ.

The work of sanctification is quiet and silent. It is wrought by the God of Peace. When God comes with power into the human spirit, there is no hurricane, tempest, fire, or earthquake, but the thrilling possession of the heart. Do not be afraid, as though God would treat us roughly. So long as peaceful, gentle methods will accomplish His purpose, He will gladly employ them.

The work is also gradual. We are not made faultless, but preserved blameless. We are kept from known sin, preserved from incurring perpetual self-reproach. "There is no condemnation." Recently I saw the love letter of a little boy to his father. It was anything but faultless; but the father, at least, did not count it worthy of blame, since he carried it next to his heart. So we are not faultless, as judged by God's perfect standard, until we are presented before the presence of His glory. But we are blameless when living within the divine will.

The work begins within and moves outwards. In the Old Testament Tabernacle, the glory of God's presence (Shechinah) shone from within the Holy of Holies, pouring light into the Holy Place, unto the outer court and beyond. In our sanctification, His presence within us will do no less.

Uncertain Riches

Charge them that are rich in this world, that they be not high-minded, nor trust in uncertain riches, but in the living God, who giveth us richly all things to enjoy. I Timothy 6:17

THE contrast here is very beautiful. Men, for the most part, look to riches to supply them with all they need richly to enjoy; but the Apostle says that it is better to look away from dead coin to a living Person, who takes pleasure in giving liberally without upbraiding.

Here is a rebuke. Suppose you had your cellars filled with gold coin, would you not feel secure against all possible need and care? Almost certainly you would. But you ought to be even more at rest, since you have neither silver nor gold, and only your Heavenly Father's hand.

Here is a contrast. Riches are uncertain at best. A man in these difficult days finds it easier to gain money than to hold it. He who is rich today may awake tomorrow to find that some sudden turn of events has made him poor. But God is not uncertain. He is the same yesterday, today, and forever. His covenants are certainties.

Here is an appeal. Trust in the living God with as much restfulness as others trust in their lands and revenues. Be glad if God takes away from you what you have clung to so tenaciously, if it has become your source of trust instead of Him. We smile at the story of the lady who was told by the captain that he had done all he could for the ship, and they must now look to the Almighty; and who replied, "O captain, has it come to that?" But we may be nearer akin to her spirit than we suppose!

Here is an assured destiny. Those who trust in riches are pierced through with many sorrows, and are caught in a materialistic hurricane. They who trust in the Lord are as Mount Zion, and cannot be shaken.

A Blessed Heritage

An inheritance incorruptible and undefiled, that fadeth not away,
reserved in heaven for you, who are kept by the power of God
through faith. I Peter 1:4,5

YES, it is an inheritance. It is a free gift, and yet we have
a right to it. We do not ask for it — we were born into
its blessed privilege. The child that lies in the cradle under
the royal family crest may claim his broad ancestral estates
simply by right of birth; and it is on that basis that the
saints hold heaven.

Oh, blessed heritage! Incorruptible! The gnawing tooth of
decay cannot injure it. Moth and rust cannot consume, nor
thieves break through to steal it. No spendthrift hand can
scatter or over-spend its treasures. Undefiled! Not a stain in
its pure robes; not a freckle on its leaves. Nothing enters
into the city that defiles or works abomination, or makes
a lie. That fadeth not away! Some of the fairest hopes that
ever blessed human vision, the most delightful friendships,
the most perfect dreams — have faded and withered before
our eyes. Our Father's heavenly inheritance never can.

It is kept for us, and we are kept for it. It is reserved in
heaven for you.

> I have a heritage of joy
>   That yet I must not see;
> The hand that bled to make it mine,
>   Is keeping it for me.

Who by the power of God are guarded through faith. We
are being brought through an enemy's country under a
strong escort, like women and children protected by a dou-
ble line of soldiers, till we are safe from danger. We are not
in heaven yet, but if we remain close to God, we are as safe
as if we were.

For the Love of Us

Who his own self bare our sins in his own body on the tree,
that we being dead to sins, should live unto righteousness.
I Peter 2:24

HE came into the sinner's world. Himself sinless, He took our nature. Accustomed to the pure atmosphere of His own bright home, He allowed His ears and eyes to be assailed by the stinging sounds and sights of men. His blessed feet trod among the dust of death, the mounds of graves, and the traps that men laid to catch Him. And all for love of us.

He lived the ordinary life of men. He labored in the carpenter's shed; attended wedding festivals and heart-rending funerals; ate, and drank, and slept. He sailed in the boat with his fisher-friends; sat wearied at the well; and was hungry with the sharp morning air.

He sympathized with the sinner's griefs. In their affliction He was afflicted. He often groaned, and sighed, and wept. When leprosy with its sores, bereavement with its heart-rending loneliness, deafness and devil-possession, came to His notice, they elicited the profoundest response from His sympathetic heart.

He died the sinner's death. He was wounded for our transgressions. He was treated as the scapegoat, the leper, the sin-offering of the human family. He stood as our substitute, sacrifice, and satisfaction. The guilt and curse and penalty of a broken law was borne and exhausted in His suffering nature.

He is preparing a home. "I go to prepare a place for you." No mother was ever more intent on preparing a bedroom for her sailor-boy on his return, than Jesus on preparing heaven for us.

Deceiving Ourselves

*If we say that we have fellowship with him, and walk in darkness,
we lie . . . If we say that we have no sin, we deceive ourselves,
and the truth is not in us.* 1 John 1:6-8

IN these passages, the beloved Apostle warns against what
we are likely to say, and indicates what would be better for
us to substitute in thought and speech.

*We sometimes say that we have fellowship with Christ,
and yet continue to walk in darkness.* It arises partly from
our desire to stand well with our fellows, or because we do
not realize how much darkness is still in our lives. But
whatever the cause, it is a lie. It is better to walk quietly
in the light, so far as we have it; and thus we shall secure
His blessed fellowship. And His blood will continually
cleanse us from sin, removing all hindrance on Christ's side
to the free communication of His choicest gifts.

Again, we sometimes say that we have no sin. It is a profound mistake on our part, arising from faulty ideas about
the nature of sin, or from ignorance of ourselves. If we
realized what God's standard of holiness and sinlessness is;
if we understood that sin consists in coming short of His
glory as much as in distinct violation of His will; if we
knew that there may be sin in motive as much as in act,
and even in want of love — we would not so speak. As
it is, we deceive ourselves, though no one else. We need to
confess our sins and obtain forgiveness through the One Ad-
vocate with the Father, Jesus Christ the Righteous.

Face to Face

*His servants shall serve him; and they shall see his face; his name
shall be in their foreheads.*   Revelation 22:3,4

THESE are the three elements in heavenly bliss:

Service. In the disciples' prayer the Lord taught us that
the will of God is done in heaven. Not that there is any in-
terruption in the perfect rest there. Activity will be as easy
and natural as the play of the bees among the limes, or of
minnows in the pool. There will be no strain, no effort, no
exhaustion. To cease those ministries which the blessed
render to Him would be intolerable pain. The disciples
would be weary with forbearing, and could not stay.

Vision. "They shall see his face." Here, through a glass
darkly; there, we shall see Him face to face. Here, as when
the two walked to Emmaus, and knew not their Companion; there, as when their eyes were opened, and they
knew Him. Oh, what a glad surprise!

Transfiguration. "His name shall be in their foreheads."
The name of God is the totality of the divine perfection and
beauty. And the bearing of His name on their foreheads indicates that they are becoming like Him, while they see Him
as He is.

There the Bible closes its record, finding man in a garden,
leaving him in a city; demonstrating that where sin reigned
unto death, there much more grace reigned through
righteousness unto eternal life, giving man a more exalted
and blessed existence than Adam ever enjoyed in Eden.